Hidden Treasures of the Disney Cruise Line

Nautical Notes, Knowledge, and Nonsense

Jim Korkis

Theme Park Press
The Happiest Books on Earth
www.ThemeParkPress.com

© 2020 Jim Korkis

No part of this publication may be reproduced, distributed, or transmitted in any form or by any means, including photocopying, recording, or other electronic or mechanical methods, without the prior written permission of the publisher, except for brief quotations embodied in critical reviews and certain other non-commercial uses permitted by copyright law.

Although every precaution has been taken to verify the accuracy of the information contained herein, no responsibility is assumed for any errors or omissions, and no liability is assumed for damages that may result from the use of this information.

Theme Park Press is not associated with the Walt Disney Company.

The views expressed in this book are those of the author and do not necessarily reflect the views of Theme Park Press.

Theme Park Press publishes its books in a variety of print and electronic formats. Some content that appears in one format may not appear in another.

Editor: Bob McLain
Layout: Artisanal Text

ISBN 978-1-68390-147-1
Printed in the United States of America

Theme Park Press | www.ThemeParkPress.com
Address queries to bob@themeparkpress.com

Dedicated to instructors Jerry Johnson, Henry Hardt and their students from Buena Vista University in Storm Lake, Iowa, who were my sometimes entertaining sailing companions on several of my voyages on the Disney Cruise Line.

Since the World Paused

This book was originally meant to be released early March 2020 but then the world paused and publication was delayed. The future of the Disney Cruise Line is open to speculation at this point in time.

Construction on DCL's second tropical destination, Lighthouse Point in the Bahamas, was stopped along with all other Disney construction which will delay completion and opening.

The Meyer Werft shipyard in Papenburg, Germany, the shipyard that builds cruise ships for Royal Caribbean, Disney Cruise Line and Carnival Corporation, said in April that several cruise lines have let them know that they won't be needing all of the new cruise ships that they previously ordered due to a slowdown in customer demand and financial losses.

As a result, the production on new cruise ships at the shipyard is being stretched out. Construction shifts have been shortened, contract staff reduced and no weekend or overtime work is scheduled. This will delay the completion date for new ships that are currently under construction.

There were four other cruise ships on the queue schedule ahead of the Disney Wish, which was due to be delivered in late 2021 and now the assumption is that the ship may be delayed up to an additional year. That will also mean the delay or cancellation of the other two Triton class ships that Disney previously ordered.

The possible extending of the use of current ships could also delay new orders even further. Both the Disney Magic and Disney Wonder were approaching their planned time for retirement but now might be rehabbed again and extended.

As owner of the shipyard, Bernard Meyer, explained, one cruise line client told him that they wouldn't need new ships, and they would just be satisfied with being able to run their current fleet. Meyer stressed the unprecedented nature of this pandemic on the industry: "Never before has the complete cruise fleet with over 400 ships stopped operating."

In mid-May, Disney CEO Bob Chapek acknowledged that DCL will likely be the last of the Disney Parks units to re-open. Among other considerations to be taken in to account will be how well local communities especially in Central Florida are able to flatten new infections, do extensive testing and strong contact tracing policies.

Of course, cruise travel would need to be considered safe enough for thousands of families to resume travel to the ports again and people having been out of work might not have the discretionary income for a cruise.

As this book goes to print, all cruises are banned until October 31, 2020 but that ban may be extended. As of July 28, all the Disney ships remain in a CDC provisionally green classification meaning they meet the surveillance criteria for "Green" status but may need to establish additional safety measures before sailing with passengers is permitted to resume.

At this time, the Disney Magic is docked in Dover, England. The Disney Fantasy is in France. The Disney Wonder and Disney Dream are docked in the vicinity of Port Canaveral.

The historical and storytelling information in this book is still accurate even if procedures may change so it was decided to publish it at this time.

Contents

Introduction ix

BEFORE THE DISNEY CRUISE LINE 1

Cruising with Walt 2

Queen Mary 6

Port Disney Sea Long Beach 10

S.S. Disney 15

The Big Red Boat 20

The Birth of DCL 28

THE DISNEY CRUISE FLEET 37

High Seas Glossary 39

Disney Magic 41

Disney Wonder 43

Disney Dream 45

Disney Fantasy 48

Captain Tom 50

The Colors of the Ship 52

Disney Cruise Line Terminal 54

Walt Disney Theater 57

Pirate Night and Fireworks 59

AquaDuck 63

Environmental Overview 65

Disney Channel Mickey Mouse Cartoons 67

Captain Minnie 68

Disney Wish 69

SEAcrets of the Ships 71

THE ART OF THE SHIP 81

Magic Portholes 82

Enchanted Art 87

The Midship Detective Agency 94

Disney Dream Elevator Art 99

Jolly Roger Steering Wheel 100

Transportation Paintings 101

Disney Nautical Cartoons 102

SEAcrets of DCL Art 104

DCL DINING 105

Disney Dream Main Dining Rooms 106

Disney Dream District Nightclubs 117

O'Gills the Lucky Fish 121

Vanellope's Sweets and Treats 124

CASTAWAY CAY 127

Castaway Cay: The Real Story 128

The Original Imagineering Back Story 130

The Revised Back Story 134

The Real "Castaways" 137

SEAcrets of Castaway Cay 138

Lighthouse Point 143

About the Author 149

More Books from Theme Park Press 151

Introduction

Ahoy and welcome aboard!

This book is NOT a travel guide nor is it designed to help get discounts, pick a good cabin, select the best time of the year to cruise, decide on a shore excursion, review the cuisine or anything else related to things that a good travel agent can help you accomplish.

There are plenty of travel guides and websites that can guide people in those matters as well as a plethora of travel consultants. This book is something different. Think of it as the "A.B. Seas" of the stories behind the Disney Cruise Line that even Disney doesn't always share with its guests.

This book recounts some of the history and storytelling about the DCL that is rarely if ever documented. In addition, this book is neither complete nor definitive but simply a compilation of some rarely known information about the DCL. As with all things Disney, things constantly change.

Disney itself states:

> Disney Cruise Line is a living experience and as such, specific events, programs and other materials are subject to change without notice and may not be available during your visit.

The ships are constantly undergoing changes from entertainment to dining to itineraries and much more so it is challenging to remain current. For instance, tours of the bridge or the galley are no longer offered although videos of those locations are shown on a channel on the stateroom television.

While the *Disney Magic* and the *Disney Wonder* have similarities and the *Disney Dream* and the *Disney Fantasy* have similarities, they have significant differences as well. Unlike some of my other books, I have occasionally included my own observations in the text where no official documentation was available for verification.

This book shares some things guests may have overlooked or never thought to ask. Disney prefers not to describe or list many of these things so that the guests can have "the joy of discovery" and so Disney cannot be held accountable for any changes or removals it may make in them.

I first set sail on the *Disney Magic* in 1998 while I was an animation instructor at the Disney Institute. In the beginning, three of us in that department (Graham Toms, Lock Wolverton and myself) were sent out individually to talk about Disney hand drawn animation, limited edition cels, Walt Disney and more backed with a visual presentation on a big screen. Graham and Lock even gave demonstrations on how to draw characters rather than lecturing all the time.

These forty-five minute long presentations were designed to offer passengers something extra and something distinctively Disney that they might not experience on cruises on other ships. Imagineers came up with the term "differentiators" to describe these offerings.

It was my first experience ever being on a cruise of any kind and it was overwhelming but delightful. I boarded as a passenger and was unloaded as cargo thanks to the never-ending food offerings. I have since learned to be more moderate in my consumption without denying myself any enjoyment.

Over two decades, I have sailed ten times on the *Disney Magic*, the *Disney Wonder* and the *Disney Dream*. I most recently cruised on the *Disney Dream* in January 2020.

I am continually impressed that the shipboard storytelling elements extend beyond just the entertainment venues and are scattered throughout the entire ship. Even with my dedicated research, personal exploration and asking questions of those who might know, I have only discovered just a fraction of what is there.

I am embarrassed to admit how many times I had visited the D Lounge on the *Disney Dream* for presentations and never noticed that the design on the carpet on the floor had script pages for Disney films like *Cinderella*, *Beauty and the Beast*, *The Lion King*, *Peter Pan*, and *Alice in Wonderland*. Since its latest rehab in dry dock, that wonderful detail is now long gone.

Or that Deck 5 near the Oceaneers Club has a lower ceiling and smaller portholes so that the children feel bigger. Or that the hallway on Deck 4 heading Aft and going toward the nightclubs uses forced perspective and less detail to make the path seem longer in order to discourage children from wandering back there.

INTRODUCTION xi

I give special thanks to Kim Eggink and Courtney Guth who each helped me find a missing puzzle piece for two of my chapters. Along with her constant support, premiere Disney fan Kim has been a long time silent angel occasionally helping me with challenging research information for my books.

There are many, many more wonderful surprises waiting to be discovered on all of the DCL ships and this book will hopefully be a good start to help answer the questions: "What am I looking at and why is it there?" Bon Voyage!

Jim Korkis
Disney Historian
June 2020

Before The Disney Cruise Line

Getting into the cruise line business was not just some out-of-the-blue decision for the Walt Disney Company but the logical extension of decades of flirting with similar ideas.

CEO Michael Eisner had a concept of a "Disney Decade" that would diversify the Walt Disney Company into other business initiatives so that it would not be so dependent on its theme parks that represented nearly 75 percent of its earnings at the time or the company's then underperforming movie division that was slowly being revitalized.

This business situation was part of the impetus to explore the possibly of a Disney cruise ship and it was not as unusual as might be assumed judging by the history of the company.

Walt Disney himself was a frequent cruise ship passenger. The Disney Studio had already produced many cartoons and live-action films that spotlighted ships including the very first theatrically released Mickey Mouse short cartoon, *Steamboat Willie* (1928).

Imagineers had proposed a floating theme park on a converted oil tanker that would sail to different ports and designed plans for a cruise ship port in Long Beach.

Disney had licensed its characters to appear on Premier Cruises' Big Red Boat and it proved so successful that it resulted in passengers extending their vacation for several days to visit Walt Disney World and stay in its resort hotels.

The following section takes a closer examination of some of those activities and how they eventually led to the creation of the Disney Cruise Line that launched in 1998. Today, it is one of the most successful business divisions of the company and will be expanding significantly within the next few years.

Cruising with Walt

By the early 1900s, steamships had replaced sailing ships as the primary way to transport people and cargo across oceans. They were relatively faster and safer. The "S.S." in front of the names of some ships designated it as a "Steampowered Ship" or simply "Steam Ship".

Steam was intially created by giant vats of boiling water that provided consistent power that didn't depend upon wind for propulsion and made ocean travel more predictable. Later, the adaptation of turbines to steam engines improved both speed and fuel efficiency. At the height of the Golden Age of Cruise Ships, it would take roughly five days to travel from New York to England.

By the early 1900s, more than ninety percent of immigrants to the United States arrived on steamships from all over the world. It was the main source of income for most passenger liners at the time and these passengers were housed on the lower steerage decks. However, they were not the only travelers.

Steamship travel was known for the opulence and high style of the first class cabins. Leisure or even business travel to Europe was an indication of wealth and prestige for many Americans. Competing cruise lines added all sorts of extravagant amenities to entice these rich passengers including palm courts, orchestras, daily news papers (printed on ship from radio news transmissions) and more.

Walt Disney would have felt quite at home on the Disney cruise ships. His early travels outside the United States including trips to the Caribbean were accomplished by the only reliable form of transportation for those journeys available during his lifetime: cruise ships.

One of his steamer trunks is on display behind glass next to his desk in the Walt Disney Presents attraction at Disney Hollywood Studios.

It was not until the mid-1960s that transatlantic flights were commonly available. They quickly gained favor for the increased speed and lower price even though they lacked the comfort and luxury of the ships. These flights eventually caused the lucrative days of cruise lines to diminish significantly resulting in many classic ships pulled out of service. The industry shifted its focus from travel to tourism.

Walt and his wife Lillian went on their first Hawaiian vacation trip from August 10 to September 1, 1934 and sailed on the Matson liner, *S.S. Lurline*. It was approximately a six-day cruise. It was their first of several visits to the Hawaiian Islands via cruise line.

Walt's first cruise experience to Europe (discounting his 1918 seafaring trip as a member of the Red Cross on a troop ship to France at the end of World War I) was a first class trip he took with his wife Lillian to England aboard the *S.S. Normandie* in 1935.

Walt and his brother Roy (with his wife Edna) had to sneak aboard through the galley in order to avoid a process server. Roy felt that the people he encountered on board were "a collection of snooty people" used to a life of privilege.

They returned from their European jaunt in July 1935 aboard the *S.S. Rex* and there are publicity photos of Walt holding a Charlotte Clark Mickey Mouse doll on deck while standing next to his wife.

At the end of Walt's South American trip in August 1941, he, along with some of his top staff, took a leisurely 17-day sea voyage from Valparaiso to New York City aboard the *Santa Clara*.

There are photos of Walt and his wife aboard the *RMS Queen Elizabeth* in November 1946 and on the same ship accompanied by their two daughters on a 1949 cruise to Europe. In addition over the years, Walt traveled on the *RMS Queen Mary, S.S. Independence* (in August 1952 with his wife and two daughters) and the *S.S. Constitution* among other ships.

The live action film *Bon Voyage* (1962) is a Disney feature film comedy featuring Fred MacMurray's character taking his family from Indiana on their first vacation to France and their many misadventures.

The film was based on a 1956 novel by Joseph and Marrijane Hayes. Joseph Hayes had previously written *The Desperate Hours* which was made into a popular Broadway play and later a film starring Humphrey Bogart. *Bon Voyage* was his second book and he and his wife wrote it after taking a trip across the Atlantic.

The movie starts with the family crossing the Atlantic Ocean on the *S.S. United States* that was withdrawn from service in 1969 but still survives today, stripped and moored at Pier 82 in Philadelphia, Pennsylvania.

Filming began using the ship on August 15, 1961 at the Hudson River pier 84 and Walt took it as an opportunity to take his family on a European vacation for the shoot. Accompanying him on the cruise was his wife, his son-in-law Ron Miller (who was an associate producer on the film) with his wife Diane and their children.

The ship with roughly 1,100 passengers sailed for five days to Le Havre. Two movies a day were shown "to capacity audiences" as part of the shipboard entertainment.

The Disney contingent included MacMurray and his wife, and actors Jane Wyman, Deborah Walley, Mickey Callan, Tommy Kirk and Kevin Corcoran. In addition, the group consisted of director James Neilson (who had directed among other Disney films *Moon-Spinners* and *Moon Pilot*), writer Bill Walsh (who also served as an associate producer and had worked on Disney films like *The Shaggy Dog* and *The Absent-Minded Professor*) and cinematropher William Snyder (who had worked on other Disney films like *Toby Tyler* and *Moon Pilot*) along with nearly fifty other members of the film crew and family members.

The United States Line who operated the ship decided that their other paying passengers had the right to a certain amount of personal privacy so established some guidelines for filming. The film crew had to be skeletal in size and had filming restricted to the first-class decks. That stipulation increased the amount of money for the production since Disney had to pay for higher priced accomodations.

Walsh complained to writer Eugene Archer of the *New York Times* in 1961, "We wanted to travel cabin class but now we have to make the character a rich carpenter." Actually the MacMurray character was made a plumbing contractor who had saved up years for the trip.

For the scenes on the ship to make the decks seem inhabited without inconveniencing the regular passengers, the Disney production used its technicians, executives and families accompanying the Disney contingent as the vacationing tourists in the shots.

Since in the screenplay the father's troubles start even before they start sailing, the film begins with the family in a taxi arriving at the pier where things are chaotic. Fifteen taxis, fifteen private cars, four studio trucks, sixty technicians, 125 extras and approximately a thousand curious sightseers produced the bedlam of trying to board a cruise ship at the time.

Jane Wyman's dressing room during the scene was actually the steamship baggage director's private office. Another scene was a disastrous and awkward going away party thrown by MacMurray's character in-laws.

When the filming in France was finished, instead of taking another cruise back to the States, the group and the equipment including a twenty-six pound Mitchell portable camera, four lighting reflectors and fifty magazines of Technicolor film used for filming on the ship were simply flown back.

Film critics did not care for the excessive length of the final film (132 minutes), its slow pacing, and the fact that the film vacillated between some adult subjects and the usual children comedy antics but didn't seem to handle either very well. The film grossed more than five million dollars at the box office and was nominated for two Academy Awards for best costume design and best sound but didn't win either.

Richard and Robert Sherman wrote the title song. Initially, they came up with a romantic waltz that others at the studio considered one of the best things they had ever composed. Walt didn't like it because he wanted something more upbeat to start the film. The Shermans were allowed to buy back their composition and composed something more glitzy to be used over the opening titles.

Richard Sherman remembered, "Walt didn't know the technical side of music, but he knew what he wanted musically. Once we wrote a sentimental waltz for the film *Bon Voyage* but when we sang it for Walt, he didn't spark to it. He said, 'That's not my song' and then burst into singing *California Here I Come*. 'That's what I want...only French!'"

The summer of 1966 before his death later that year, Walt gathered his entire family together for a thirteen day cruise up the coast of British Columbia on a 140 foot chartered yacht, where the family celebrated not only one of his granddaughter's birthdays, but Walt and Lillian's wedding anniversary.

While his sons-in-law would go salmon fishing in a little dinghy, Walt spent quiet time on the deck reading books about city planning in preparation for Epcot and books about colleges in preparation for California Institute of the Arts.

Ron Miller, Diane Disney's husband, described Walt as "serene" during the cruise, even though it rained during much of the time.

Being serene on a cruise was atypical for Walt because, as his daughter, Diane Disney Miller remembered, "on a ship in the middle of the ocean, [Walt] would go out of his mind. He couldn't find enough to do. On one trip, he got in a shuffleboard tournament with Catholic priests who were returning from a pilgrimage."

Queen Mary

How did Disney end up operating the fabled cruise liner the *Queen Mary* in Long Beach from 1988 to 1992? The short answer is that Disney CEO Michael Eisner wanted to own the Disneyland Hotel.

The British cruise ship RMS *Queen Mary* sailed the North Atlantic Ocean from England to New York and back as the flagship of the Cunard Line from 1936 to 1940 when it was transformed into a troop ship during World War II.

In 1947, the ship was refitted as a passenger ship and dominated the transatlantic crossings until the introduction of faster transatlantic flights that could make the trip in hours rather than days resulting in the ship operating at a loss. It sometimes came into port with more crew members than passengers. It was retired in 1967.

It was purchased by the city of Long Beach in California for $3.45 million dollars and, since it was too large to sail through the Panama Canal, it journeyed around the South American Cape Horn to arrive in Long Beach where it was moored. After a long conversion from a sea going vessel to a hotel, museum and tourist attraction, it opened to the public in May 1971. It was now officially classified as a building rather than a ship.

Different operators were handling different aspects of the attraction and, as a result, it was losing millions of dollars for the city each year. In 1980, the Long Beach's Port Harbor Commission assigned a 66-year lease to Wrather Port Properties Corporation in the hopes that having just one operator might turn things around.

It was run by Jack Wrather, an entrepreneur who owned such intellectual properties as the Lone Ranger, Lassie, Sergeant Preston of the Yukon, as well as the Disneyland Hotel among other investments.

From 1983 to 1993, the *Queen Mary* was joined nearby by a huge geodesic dome that housed Howard Hughes' infamous

H-4 Hercules aircraft, colloquially known as the Spruce Goose because it was made of wood.

Wrather and his wife were friends with Walt Disney and so Walt asked him to build the Disneyland Hotel in 1954.

Wrather also knew, like Walt, that Anaheim was primed for major expansion. Walt was so desperate to have a hotel nearby for guests to stay when they visited his park that he gave Wrather a 99-year lease on the land that Disney had purchased across from the park (at a rate of $2,000 a year for the length of the lease, plus 2% of the gross on the rentals) and the exclusive rights to use the "Disney" name for the hotel and any future hotels that Wrather might build in Southern California (at a rate of $25,000 per year) and Walt's assurance that he would not build a hotel in competition with Wrather.

When Michael Eisner became CEO in September 1984, one of the things that irritated him was that there was a hotel called the Disneyland Hotel that Disney did not own. Even worse, it was falling into disrepair, which reflected badly on the Disney Brand.

Eisner also coveted the acreage around the hotel and was upset that he was prevented from building other competing hotels in the Southern California area.

Jack Wrather died in November 1984. In March 1987, Disney negotiators tried to make a deal to buy out the Wrather Corporation, but offered $6 less a share than the stock was selling for at the time.

In June 1987, a New Zealand firm purchased 28% of Wrather Corporation and announced it intended to eventually purchase at least 50%. This meant a foreign company might gain control of the Disneyland Hotel and the right to use the "Disney" name on any other hotels in Southern California.

Disney approached the New Zealand firm for a joint buy-out of Wrather in a deal that cost Disney $76 million dollars in 1988. Six months later, Disney purchased that firm's 50% interest in Wrather for an additional $85 million.

In total, it cost Disney $161 million to gain control of the Disneyland Hotel, plus the assumption of an additional $89 million in debts that Wrather had generated.

That same package included the contracts and leases for the *Queen Mary* and the Spruce Goose, as well as the Londontowne

Village, which was a collection of quaint shops and restaurants between the plane and the ship.

Wrather also had had an option to lease about 236 acres near the *Queen Mary* that could be developed as a marina or filled in to create land that could be used for a retail district.

Disney created a subsidiary company, WCO Port Properties, to oversee the Long Beach property lease. Those who worked for the company were given their own special WCO (Walt Disney Company) Port Properties nametags.

Disney didn't officially promote the entertainment complex as a Disney venue, but it did try to make it profitable. Disney created a popular Haunted Passage tour for the *Queen Mary*, as well as other limited capacity tours, like Celebrity Tales, that took guests through areas where the rich and famous stayed, and Legendary Passages, which followed in the steps of a typical crossing.

Disney hired look-alike performers of famous celebrities who might have sailed on the *Queen Mary* in its heyday like W.C. Fields, The Marx Brothers, Mae West, and Clark Gable to wander the ship and interact with guests. A Howard Hughes impersonator gave tours of the Spruce Goose and shared its history.

Newly restored staterooms and suites at the *Queen Mary* were available for overnight accommodations. Disney upgraded the restaurants and shops. Harrods, the famous London department store opened its first "Signature Store" in the United States aboard the Queen Mary on January 5, 1989.

Jack Lindquist, then executive vice president of creative marketing concepts for Walt Disney Attractions, pulled out all the bells and whistles for 1990 with a year long celebration in an attempt to attract a larger audience. By now the *Queen Mary* had 15 specialty shops, 17 snack bars, three full-service restaurants, and Sir Winston's piano bar.

For the promotion, Disney expected visitors to feel as if they have been transported back to 1939. Daily live shows evoked the era with on-board performers entertaining the passengers.

The *Queen Mary* and Spruce Goose Entertainment Center hosted the "Voyage to 1939" celebration to reference the ship's last peacetime voyage on August 30, 1939 before it was converted into a troop transport carrier.

The celebration was held every day "Rain or Shine" from January 6 to December 31, 1990. It ended with a gigantic New

Year's Eve Gala on December 31 "when we bid fond farewell to the 1930s," Lindquist said.

Among the onboard festivities were a musical tour of the ship, a "preview" of a 1930s style New York revue with live entertainers entitled the "Bon Voyage Party" with music from "Hollywood's Heyday and Broadway's Ballyhoo".

In addition, Big Band music for dancing in a special Club 39 decorated like a popular nightclub of the era was available. Cast members roamed the ship in period costumes and interacted with guests in the persona of 1939 passengers on a cruise.

Each day, visitors were presented with newspaper front pages from the same date in 1939. As they toured, they heard specially prepared tapes with authentic newscasts, sports results and music as the ship's radio broadcasts.

On shore starting in April, an Old English carnival called the Brighton Carnival took over the Londontowne Village shopping/dining complex with authentic English food and drink. It also featured children's rides and carnival games in an attempt to make the area family friendly.

Disney offered special promotions to get people to the entertainment complex. Flyers were handed out at Disneyland offering $3 off each admission to the *Queen Mary* for up to 10 people. At one point, Disneyland guests were offered free admission to the Long Beach attraction with a paid admission to Disneyland.

It quickly became apparent that people visiting Disneyland, especially for multiple days, had no desire to take the trip out to Long Beach. The venue struggled financially.

In an effort to make the acquisition profitable, Disney announced in 1990 that the two icons of the *Queen Mary* and Spruce Goose would be the centerpiece for a new elaborate theme park to be called Port Disney (and later DisneySea). When the plans for that Long Beach project fell through and with a survey that identified at least $27 million in needed repairs for the ship alone, Disney decided to abandon the lease and the venue in March 1992. It would continue to operate the attractions until September 30, the end of the fiscal year.

The *Queen Mary* is still owned by the city of Long Beach, but it's operated by a real estate firm, Urban Commons, that has announced its intention to build a $250 million entertainment complex for the 65 acres of waterfront surrounding the *Queen Mary*.

Dubbed "Queen Mary Island," the sprawling project will include cafes, bars, a 2,400-foot-long boardwalk, a 200-room hotel and nearly 700,000 square feet of retail space, plus an amphitheater and an advanced playground area for extreme sports. The complex could also incorporate an "ice climbing wall," as well as surfing, skydiving, and zip lining.

Port Disney Sea Long Beach

In 1990, the Walt Disney Company almost built a five berth port in Long Beach, California that would have provided access for cruise ships. It would actually have been the largest cruise terminal on the west coast at that time if it had been built.

It was just one small part of a much larger project known as Port Disney and later DisneySea that was part of then CEO Michael Eisner's announced "Disney Decade" that was a series of expansion plans that would have included building a new theme park to be located either in Anaheim (basically on the area of the Disneyland parking lot along with some additional acreage) or in Long Beach.

Since such an entertainment venue was guaranteed to bring in millions of dollars in tax revenue and additional jobs, the final location would be based on which proposed city provided the major concessions the company wanted to help facilitate the construction and make major modifications to the existing infrastructure including significant road improvements.

For Anaheim, Disney proposed WestCot, a variation of its East Coast Epcot theme park. For Long Beach, the concept of a Port Disney was first presented to city and port officials in closed meetings in July 1990 and then officially announced in a public meeting on July 31.

The property would have had a nautical-themed park known as DisneySea (no space between the two words), a marina, a cruise ship port (potentially competing with the existing Port of Los Angeles for cruise ship traffic) and an expanded specialty retail and entertainment area in addition to five resort hotels,

The new themed venue would reportedly cost more than $2.8 billion. In October 1991, the entire Port Disney project would be renamed DisneySea to avoid complaints that there would be confusion with the Port of Long Beach.

While the plans were eventually scuttled, many of the things developed for the Port Disney project were later incorporated into Japan's Tokyo DisneySea theme park (that opened in 2001) so obviously the development of attractions had been far enough along for the Oriental Land Company to review them and decide to pursue that "seven seas" concept for their second park as early as 1992.

Representatives from neighborhood associations and businesses in Long Beach objected to the significantly increased traffic concerns, the public subsidies that Disney demanded that were felt to be excessive, environmental concerns and other issues.

Surprised by this cool reception, Disney did a huge publicity push emphasizing that they would be a good neighbor and the project was important to the city.

In addition, Disney published one issue of *The Port Disney News* filled with elaborate and colorful concept art and detailed descriptions, which was mailed directly to residents of Long Beach in 1991 in the hopes of addressing any concerns and stirring up support for the project.

According to its designers, the goal of DisneySea was to enable everyone to experience the marvels of nature's secret world beneath the sea and to gain first-hand experience of how the oceans affect human life as well as the life of the planet.

The Port Disney resort complex would span roughly 414 acres on both sides of Queensway Bay. The two sides of the resort, known as City-Side and Port-Side, would be connected by watercraft, monorail and the Queensway Bridge.

City-Side would be the location of three Disney resort hotels, shopping and entertainment areas and would integrate existing facilities like the Hyatt Regency Hotel, the Long Beach Convention Center, Shoreline Village and the Downtown Long Beach Marina.

Port Disney's monorail system would run alongside Shoreline Drive, and connect with these three Disney hotels. Disney would build two more resort hotels on Port-Side.

The WorldPort (no separation between words) just outside the theme park on Port-Side would be the location where excursion water ferries would depart on a regular basis to Avalon, Newport Beach, Dana Point, Redondo Beach and Marina del Rey. It would have a promenade that provided easy access to shops and restaurants and would be the end of the monorail line.

It was suggested that theme boats, pageants and special events would be featured in the area where the *Queen Mary* would also now be docked as a familiar visual icon. In addition, at night there would be laser and fireworks shows.

In order to justify the need for 250 acres of landfill, Disney had to include marinas, a cruise ship port, ferry ports and even some sort of an aquarium in order to meet the requirements of the Coastal Commission.

One of the things that made the DisneySea theme park different than Disneyland was that it was specifically to be educationally oriented, in addition to the entertainment aspects, much like the original overall intent of Epcot Center in Florida or the Living Seas pavilion at Epcot.

Without an iconic castle, the centerpiece for the park would have been Oceana, a series of six bubble-shaped structures that interlocked and would have been balanced on a podium of diagonally thrusting rockwork. One design had the monorail passing through the largest of Oceana's bubbles.

The largest sphere would house a huge water ride where guests would travel in spherical capsules through the evolution of the seas and past many different underwater habitats including a volcano, dark ocean trenches and freezing ice caps.

It would house the world's largest "oceanarium," a two-story aquarium reaching depths of up to thirty feet and holding ten to twelve million gallons of water and an extensive learning center. It would have had hands-on experiences where guests could learn the power of a tsunami and operate giant crab claws.

In fact, Oceana would house the Future Research Center that was to be a working meeting center for oceanographic researchers, as well as the Ocean Outreach Center described as a "library of the sea."

It would have been a massive research library, an "Exploratorium of Knowledge", dedicated to all aspects of the ocean throughout the world with computers, reading rooms, research files, and full access to ocean-centric literature for everyone from guests to scientists.

It was hoped that respected scientists from around the world would visit to conduct studies because of the vastness of the available resources and make themselves available occasionally to answer guests' questions.

For the average guest there would be interactive exhibits to learn about the ocean and marine life, a submarine simulator named the Nautilus 2000 going to various underwater locations and even an exhibit to demonstrate how to clean up an oil spill.

Overhead walkways and underwater portholes would provide views of the marine creatures. Kids would be able to borrow goggles that allowed them to appreciate what it was like to see as a fish.

Just as Disneyland had several different lands, there were several different sections of DisneySea:

Mysterious Island: The icon of this section was a man-made volcano and the area centered around stories of Captain Nemo and his Nautilus submarine. It featured several attractions, including Pirate Island (described as "Tom Sawyer's Island times 10" where supervised by Disney's buccaneers, children could follow clues that would lead to a buried treasure), Nemo's Lava Cruiser (where suspended guests in ore carts would careen through underground caverns in the volcano that would eventually erupt with a blast of steam) and the Lost City of Atlantis (a gentle boat ride taking guests on a twisting route through the remains of the lost civilization's crystalline passages while barely avoiding threatening whirlpools, volcanic eruptions and an encounter with a sea monster).

Heroes' Harbor: This area was themed as an ancient Greek village where "the myths and legends of the sea come to life." It featured attractions like the Aqua-Labyrinth that was a "challenging maze with walls made only of water," a ride that was to based on the voyages of Sinbad the Sailor and another attraction centering on the adventures of Ulysses from Homer's famous poem.

Fleets of Fantasy: Near the boardwalk area, it was described by Disney as "a harbor of fabled and fanciful ships, including outsized Chinese junks and Egyptian galleys that would disguise exciting rides and dining and entertainment experiences."

Venture Reefs: This area, originally known as "Adventure Reefs," seemed reminiscent of Florida's Typhoon Lagoon water park. Guests had the opportunity to surf or snorkel through tropical reefs filled with fish where guests might explore sunken ships for pirate treasure or just enjoy the paradise-like setting and swim. One piece of concept art shows guests being lowered in a steel cage into a tank of sharks. Guests would enjoy scenic beach vistas from the Caribbean, Polynesian, and the Pacific. Guests would dine and shop in one of the main areas of the park designated for those activities.

Boardwalk and Rainbow Pier: Designed as a tribute to Long Beach's famous Pike amusement park, this area would include a Ferris Wheel and an old-fashioned wooden roller coaster with crisscrossed beams.

Such a massive undertaking could not be done all at once, so Disney announced that like Walt Disney World, the park would open in two phases. The first phase would be operating by the year 2000 with the second and final phase completed by 2010. Disney officially cancelled the project in December 1991 and announced it would instead proceed with the Anaheim WestCot proposal.

The following reasons have been cited for the cancellation:

- A special bill would have needed to be passed by California to permit Disney to proceed with the landfill and allow recreational use of the new property.
- Disney would have had to also restore wetlands elsewhere at a significant cost to mitigate the marine environmental impact and couldn't come to an agreement on the amount of land to be restored.
- Significant financial overruns for the EuroDisneyland project in France drained working capital forcing not only the abandonment of this project but also eventually WestCot in Anaheim.
- The City of Long Beach was greatly divided about the project, as well as the money it would need to contribute to do things like improvements to the Long Beach Freeway and other roads because of all the additional traffic.

S.S. Disney

On May 3, 1994, Disney announced that they intended to start their own cruise line with operations starting as early as 1998 which was the year the *Disney Magic* did indeed launch.

However, briefly before starting its own cruise line, Disney considered a floating theme park on a ship to be christened the *S.S. Disney*.

Jim Cora of Disneyland International (first as vice president and then later chairman) had been involved with the opening of Tokyo Disneyland and later Euro Disney (Disneyland Paris) Resort. He was attending a fundraising dinner as a representative of the Disney Company in 1992 and was seated next to a U.S. Navy admiral, who, during the general good spirits of the evening and the abundant cocktails jokingly proposed an unusual offer to Cora.

He mentioned that he had a spare aircraft carrier that Disney was more than welcome to build a theme park on. Cora realized it was a joke and laughed appropriately, but later that night gave the idea some further thought as a possibility of tapping into a wider international audience that might never be able to travel to a Disney theme park.

In addition, from his experience, it was expensive to build a Disney theme park in a foreign country and there were many challenges dealing with local regulations, culture and populations.

The next morning he pitched the idea of a floating Disney theme park that would travel for short periods to different countries to his staff who all loved the idea. Cora then decided to investigate if there was anyone at Disney who might know enough about ships to determine whether the idea was actually feasible.

Larry Fink, who worked with Imagineer Mark Hickson on Disneyland's Splash Mountain, knew about Hickson's thirteen years of shipbuilding experience and told Cora that Hickson would be the man for the job.

Hickson started his career at WDI in February 1988 working on the Splash Mountain project for Disneyland, and then became part of the Tokyo Disneyland project as well as contributing to that park's future master planning.

Over the years, Hickson had been involved in over 30 Disney projects that included the TDL version of Splash Mountain; Disneyland's ToonTown; the new Spaceship Earth show at Epcot;

the 3-D film *Honey, I Shrunk the Audience*; Epcot Interactive Fountain; and Innoventions; as well as other Disney projects, like the Broadway production of *Beauty and the Beast* and Disneyland's 35th Birthday celebration.

Hickson was well-versed on both ships and producing Disney attractions. Cora called and talked about the feasibility of using an aircraft carrier as the base for a floating theme park. Hickson immediately responded that it would be better to use a larger craft, like a cargo ship or an oil tanker, because of the flexibility and having a much greater capacity. Finally, a super tanker was agreed on as the base.

Cora pitched the idea to CEO Michael Eisner and Frank Wells who both loved the idea. They were working under the assumption that the upcoming opening of Euro Disney Resort in 1992 would generate an influx of capital for several new projects in what was called the Disney Decade.

Hickson was put in place as project manager and technical director for the project. He was in charge of developing the concept and doing feasibility studies. Concept architects, show designers, script writers, concept artists and model makers worked under his supervision for nine months putting together the plans for the project that also resulted in the creation of a model that could be taken apart to reveal each of the five decks.

Jan Sircus was the lead concept architect on the *S.S Disney* and then later moved on to developing "location based entertainment" concepts like Disney Quest for the company.

The idea was to bring the Disney experience and promote the Disney brand in countries where the company would never consider building a permanent theme park for a variety of reasons like expense and lack of potential continual attendance.

The WDI team looked at different locations internationally that had a port that could handle such a large super-sized vessel as well as what type of attractions might appeal to such different cultures.

As Hickson told author Alain Littaye who has done extensive documentation of the project:

> Thanks to the super tanker's architecture, the cavernous volume inside the ship gave us the opportunity to put four to five decks of attractions inside plus more attractions on the top deck. We were

looking at 16 to 18 attractions, about half of what would be at a Disney theme park.

In addition, they had to consider whether there was enough surrounding room and access at each port for the expected attendance that was estimated at 10,000 to 20,000 people a day, about a fourth or less of the guests that might attend a traditional Disney theme park.

Primarily, the WDI team looked at possibilities of the ship traveling to Europe, South America, Southeast Asia, Australia, and the Mediterranean. Later the focus initially narrowed to the West Pacific, which included the port cities of Seoul, Beijing, Shanghaî, Canton, Hong Kong, Taiwan, Manila, Djakarta, and Singapore.

Other ports investigated included Australia (Sydney, Brisbane, Melbourne), Dubai, Cape Town, and even Honolulu.

The plan was for the ship to stay in a port for two to three months and then travel to the next location. It would not return to a port for four to five years so that would build anticipation, as well as make the experience something more special, prompting people to come and visit during the limited time or miss out for half a decade.

Actually, it would not just be just one ship but a "Disney navy" fleet of three ships. The floating theme park, another smaller vessel that would be able to shoot off night time fireworks show in the middle of the harbor (since it would have been unsafe to fire them from the main vessel) and a passenger ship for the permanent staff since there would not be facilities to house them on the main ship in addition to the concerns about safety issues.

Instead of flying the cast members to each port and then boarding them in local hotels, the decision was to purchase a used passenger ship that would accompany the main vessel.

Half of the staff for the theme park including operations cast members, maintenance, technical and more would be permanent while the other half would be temporary and hired and trained in each location and supervised during the months in port by the "senior" staff.

The "junior" staff would go through roughly two weeks of training before the arrival of the boat and needed to be conversational (not necessarily fluent) in English just like the International program at Epcot, as well as fluent in the local language. WDI did some surveys in possible ports and determined there would be a large labor pool of young people interested in temporarily working for Disney.

The entrance area on the dock would have been what was described as a "portable main gate" that could be assembled from themed containers. The containers would be shipped in advance to the dock side location and assembled to become a ticketing plaza with booths selling tickets, souvenirs and food that would be in operation before the arrival of the *S.S. Disney* to start to create the Disney experience and build excitement.

It was decided to divide the opening and closing of the park into two half-days at eight hours each. That would be 10,000 guests in the morning/early afternoon and another 10,000 guests in the late afternoon/evening.

The center or "Hub" of the ship that the guests entered had a big glass canopy over the top of it. In addition to gigantic elevators and escalators to help guests access the different levels, there were emergency evacuation stairways located next to them.

The planned attractions would primarily be from Fantasyland and Tomorrowland. It was felt that Main Street USA, Frontierland and Adventureland were generally more "American-centric" and would not be interesting to a wide cultural audience.

One of the factors in determining which attractions to use also depended upon limited wait time so that it was possible for most guests to experience most attractions within the eight hour time limit.

On the top deck there was the Orbitron, a Fantasyland Carrousel under a glass dome, Casey Jr. Train (that would loop around the carrousel), a large Ferris Wheel (that would have exterior armatures that would collapse toward the deck when the ship sailed to another port so it was not sticking up high in the air), Alice in Wonderland's spinning Tea Cups and Dumbo the Flying Elephant.

At the stern end of the top deck, there would be the "it's a small world" ride, but this attraction would not have used a water flume but omnimover vehicles on a bus-bar track similar to the ones in attractions like The Haunted Mansion, because it was decided that using water would have been a challenge.

Under the Orbitron would have been a futuristic multi-story themed sit-down restaurant. There was only one restaurant as such, because the Imagineers did not want guests to spend too much time sitting down and eating during their limited eight-hour stay.

There would also be six themed fast food locations near retail shops that sold primarily Fantasyland and Tomorrowland themed merchandise. Most of the food and beverage, as well as most of the retail locations, on each deck were initially located around the midship area for efficiency in service as well as being easier to locate.

In addition, there would be a Disney Store and an Art of Disney gallery store.

Other decks included an Aladdin dark ride with a faux rock work entrance reminiscent of the Cave of Wonders and nearby the flying carpet Dumbo-style spinner attraction. The area also had a Little Mermaid dark ride with the entrance being Prince Eric's village. It was a suspended gondola attraction like Peter Pan's Flight mimicking floating underneath the ocean.

One deck had a small ToonTown area with Mickey Mouse's house primarily to facilitate meet and greet opportunities with Mickey and other characters, as well as some interactive play areas including a treehouse.

Also in the area was Roger Rabbit's Car Toon Spin (with a small fountain in front) and a 3-D movie theatre with a balcony that would show either *Muppet*Vision 3-D* or a new show featuring *The Lion King* characters, among other show possibilities proposed.

Simulator attractions included Star Tours and a *20,000 Leagues under the Sea* experience.

An oil tanker ship was so big and deep that there were plans for an iron roller coaster like Space Mountain inside down below the decks. However, since there was no actual mountain structure, the attraction would have been renamed.

Eisner pushed for the roller coaster to be themed to Indiana Jones and based on the scene from the film *Indiana Jones and the Temple of Doom* with the runaway ore car. It would have been done like a traditional "wild mouse" ride similar in structure to the Primeval Whirl attraction at Disney's Animal Kingdom.

Additional plans included a large pipe organ that would play music, a giant retro-telescope and a mini-castle, among other ideas that were never finalized.

Besides the attractions, the ship also had maintenance shops, a large central kitchen to supply food to the guest locations, waste treatment plants, storage areas and more. There was also an entertainment staging area for the singers, dancers, musicians and costumed characters who would roam the ship and perform.

While both Michael Eisner and Frank Wells loved the project, Disney company losses on Euro Disneyland—which resulted in the cancellation of several Disney Decade projects—and the death of Wells put a damper on the project.

The strategic planning group at corporate convinced Eisner that just concentrating on doing a Disney themed cruise ship would be easier, less maintenance, less expensive and more profitable.

Among the arguments were that that salt air would cause damage to the exposed attractions on the upper deck. Different countries had different safety standards as well as requirements for entertainment venues so legal issues could result. Sufficient sewage transfer access might not be available in some ports, at least for something the size of a floating theme park.

Constant maintenance not just on the attractions but on the ship itself would increase the costs. The area was limited so it was not expandable should demand increase beyond expectations. How expensive would it be to replace existing attractions inside the ship? Would medical facilities be necessary?

Would enough profit be generated without the Disney resort hotels that funnel so much additional money to support the theme parks? Would there be enough parking available at each location that would be dedicated to Disney for the three month docking?

All of these challenges and more made it an easy decision at the time to shelve the project and shift the focus to creating the Disney Cruise Line. So the *S.S. Disney* quietly sunk out of sight to join so many other proposed but never built Disney projects.

The Big Red Boat

From 1985 to 1992, Disney partnered with Premier Cruise Line and its primary cruise ship, The Big Red Boat (so-called because of the bright red color on its hull) that operated out of Cape Canaveral, Florida to provide Disney costumed characters for the short cruises to the Bahamas in connection with a multi-day vacation stay at Walt Disney World.

When Michael Eisner came on board in 1984 as CEO, he saw that the cruise line industry was growing, especially in Florida where Walt Disney World was located.

However, the Disney Company was coming out of a period where its finances were at its lowest ebb due to having had to pay out a huge sum to avoid a hostile take-over as well as producing low-performing films. It could not afford the hundreds of millions of dollars it would take to build its own ship and get into the business.

Just as Eisner partnered with an outside company to build the Swan and Dolphin resort hotels on Disney property to better understand how it was done and what it would take so that he could then build his own, Eisner also decided to partner with a cruise line.

Disney partnered with Norwegian Caribbean Lines for a November 3 -10, 1984 FantaSea Cruise out of Miami to St. Thomas, the Virgin Islands, Nassau and the Great Stirrup Cay in the Bahamas.

Disney costumed characters like Mickey Mouse, Minnie, Donald Duck and Goofy were on board to interact with passengers even at breakfast dining. All of the S.S. Norway's regular entertainment and shows were replaced by Disney's entertainers in their own productions including a live action version of Pirates of the Caribbean, a Goofy themed Olympics on deck, an Epcot International Night and a Fantasy in the Sky evening fireworks display.

During the cruise, Disney film classics were shown as well as a special hook-up with the new Disney Channel available on the on-board televisions in every cabin. Rates for the cruise ranged from $1,095 to $2,710 per person, double occupancy.

Also in 1984, Premier Cruise Line teamed with Eastern Airlines, "The Official Airline of Walt Disney World", to provide airfare to Central Florida and to offer the Premier Cruise and Disney Week on the *S.S. Royale* out of Cape Canaveral.

The experiment was enough of a success so that the following year Premier became the Official Cruise Line of Walt Disney World offering special vacation packages. Guests could choose three or four nights in a Walt Disney World resort paired with a three or four night cruise out of nearby Port Canaveral.

The package included round trip airfare, free seven day rental car with unlimited mileage, admission to all the WDW theme parks, accommodations at a Walt Disney World resort or one of the nearby less expensive good neighbor resort hotels, and admission with a free guided tour of NASA Kennedy Space Center's Spaceport USA.

Print and television ads and even material supplied by the Walt Disney Travel Company prominently featured Disney costume characters on the ships with many images of them interacting at different times with the guests from dining to recreational activities. In actuality, the characters did not appear as often as guests expected. Think of them as a condiment that was sparingly added occasionally.

S.S. *Oceanic* built in 1965 by Cantieri Riuniti dell'Adriatico in Monfalcone Italy was part of the Home Lines cruise ships and originally meant for transatlantic cruises. At 39,241 gross registered tons, it could accommodate over 1,200 passengers and was 782 feet long with a beam of 97 feet.

However transatlantic flights severely crippled the transatlantic cruise business at the time so the ship instead sailed at 95 percent capacity or less doing seven-day cruises from New York to the Bahamas and extended Caribbean cruises in the winter.

In 1982, *Oceanic* lost her position as the flagship of the Home Lines when the line received the newer S.S. *Atlantic* and had an order for another ship that was slated to arrive in 1985 and take over *Oceanic*'s itineraries. So, after twenty years of service, it was sold to Premier Cruise Line that had been formed in 1983 and wanted to establish itself as a short cruise experience for the entire family.

The ship underwent an extensive refit where much of the interior was transformed from ocean liner elegant to more of a mass market style. Premier's research showed that many of those who went on cruises out of Miami came from the Central Florida area so leaving from Cape Canaveral would make more sense as well as offer the opportunity to experience the many local Central Florida amusements.

By repainting the *Oceanic*'s hull a bright red, it distinguished the ship as different and more fun especially for young families. It advertised itself as an "incredible floating family resort". Premier marketed the ship as The Big Red Boat.

While other cruise lines allowed children on board, The Big Red Boat was the first to actively welcome them as part of the experience.

Bruce Nierenberg began his career with Norwegian Cruise Lines in 1973 but had bigger dreams. As he recalled in 2007:

> By 1983 the urge to start my own cruise line had a hold on me. My personal challenge was to figure out how to create a new line that could survive without having to compete with the others head to head.
>
> The key was differentiation. For example, I opted for Port Canaveral as our home port. My colleagues thought I was crazy, but I saw the potential to reach a much larger drive-to audience than Miami could attract, and I liked being the only cruise line in town. We also had proximity to Orlando with Walt Disney World. When we purchased the *Oceanic*, she was christened by Minnie Mouse. It made the cover of the *New York Times*.
>
> Premier Cruise Lines became the most successful tour operator in Florida, selling the most Disney tickets, using the most hotel rooms and renting the most cars. For a while, Premier was the leading three- and four-day cruise line. We were the first cruise line to commit to family cruising year-round, with a staff of 30 plus youth counselors onboard and programs for kids divided by age groups.
>
> We developed the first children's menus and provided free onboard babysitting. And the big draw: We had Disney characters in costume on board. We created experiences for the passengers, not just an onboard environment. With our beach parties and emphasis on onboard personalities, we provided a total immersion in the cruise experience that is missing from many cruise ships today. Kids were really welcome for the first time.

The success of The Big Red Boat did indeed lead the major cruise lines to position ships to Port Canaveral. In the first year of its partnership with Disney, over 60,000 passengers embarked on the cruises and the partnership was also having a significant increase on Premier's non-Disney cruises as well.

After the contract with Disney was not renewed, Premier then licensed Warner Brothers cartoon characters like Bugs Bunny and Pepe le Pew for its ships to keep its family friendly image, but continued to offer Walt Disney World/cruise packages.

The Premier line introduced two new Big Red Boats (also older refitted ships) in 1998 but the company went bankrupt in September 2000. The ships were sold to other companies with the *Oceanic* sailing until 2012 when it was scrapped. The two other Big Red Boats had been sold for scrap in 2005.

There is some speculation why the contract was not renewed. Some have suggested that Disney increased the fee of the licensing to the point that it was no longer financially viable for Premier and may have wanted to control other aspects.

Others suggest Disney was having concerns that the general public was seeing these ships as "Disney's ships" but other than the handful of character appearances, Disney was not involved in any part of the experience, including accommodations, food or entertainment that might not match the expected Disney quality and attention to detail.

From January to November 1992, The Disney Company tried to partner unsuccessfully with both Carnival Cruise Line and Royal Caribbean Cruise Line for a more upscale package with greater Disney participation.

Eisner had now seen how it all operated and with the Disney Company now on a strong financial foundation, Disney could keep all the money "in house" rather than sharing it with an outside partner and be in complete control if it went into the cruise line business.

After all, Eisner reasoned, Disney was already providing hotel accommodations, entertainment, food service, guest service and more. The only thing missing was the ship so Disney announced the launching of the Disney Cruise Line.

Advertising during the Premier years declared:

> The Big Red Boat. She'll bring you closer and closer…to each other. The Official Cruise Line of Walt Disney World is America's premier family vacation experience. It's the Bahamas, the Sea, and Walt Disney World, in seven wonderful days that last a lifetime. If you miss being a family, don't miss The Big Red Boat.
>
> Through the eyes of a child, The Big Red Boat is a fairy tale come to life—a shiny red boat of wondrous proportions and endless surprises.

For adults, the ship featured cabarets, casinos (something that was originally considered for the Disney Cruise Line but vetoed by Eisner), nightclubs, theaters, informal piano bars and lounges, health clubs, swimming pools, whirlpools, exclusive boutiques, and duty-free shops among other things.

The Big Red Boat offered the SeaSport fitness program supervised by trained instructors. The gyms featured equipment from Nautilus, Universal and Lifecycle. Offered were aerobic classes, exercise sessions, open-air jogging track on deck, pools, massage rooms and more.

For kids, they had their own kids' recreation center, Teen Nite Club, state-of-the-art video arcade, supervised activities, special programs, their own pools, ice-cream parlors and "friends their own age to share in the excitement".

There were four separate programs of kids' activities divided by age group so that younger children played with their peers and bigger kids were offered different agendas.

Each child received their own daily activities sheet for making individual choices like making a visit to the Captain's bridge. The schedule lasted until 10pm each day. A group babysitting was available for a nominal fee in the evenings for kids 2 and older.

First Mates were children aged 2-4 years old and they had their own club, Pluto's Playhouse with a kiddie pool, slides and play equipment. Youth counselors read stories, led sing-a-longs and helped with "artistic expression" activities.

Kids Call was for children 5-7 years old and some of the same First Mates activities overlapped like a treasure hunt on the deserted island as well as sharing Pluto's Playhouse. However, Kids Call had some of its own things to do like the Guppies program teaching about the wonders of the sea and the special dance party with the Disney characters as well as toys and games.

Star Cruisers were for children 8—12 years old. Their schedule included a shipboard Scavenger Quest and Shipmates Signature Search as well as the Nintendo Sports Challenge.

Teen Cruisers were for children 13 and older. They had a roster of special daily activities as well as access to the Teen Nite Club and water sports like windsurfing and the Splashdown snorkeling program on Salt Cay.

Premier was the first cruise line to create accommodations designed especially for families with four and five berth staterooms so families could cruise together economically and offered a "Kids' Quarters" second stateroom just for the kids at far less than the regular rate. Premier even offered the first single-parent plan in the cruise travel industry.

There were two exclusive Bahamas itineraries: Nassau and uninhabited Salt Cay or Abacos Out Islands with its glorious beaches and quaint fishing villages.

The ship anchored at Nassau for a day's adventure and then moved on according to the travel brochure to the powdery-white sands of the "uninhabited Salt Cay which you may just recognize as the setting for *Gilligan's Island* and more recently, the Touchstone movie *Splash*. Rumor has it that Salt Cay once harbored a band of pirates!"

Passengers were given big beach towels and indulged in pedal boating, sun canoeing, shell hunting, tubing, basketball and beach volleyball games, swimming, relaxing in hammocks strung between palm trees, enjoying a calypso band and more on the five beaches that ringed the island. There was a traditional Bahamas barbecue with char-grilled chicken, burgers, tropical fruit and more.

One of the kids' activities was to locate under the direction of the counselors the missing cruise director who's been kidnapped by "angry" pirates.

The Abacos Out Islands cruise took guests to the Green Turtle Cay (once one of the largest settlements in the Bahamas) with the typical museum and shops; Man-O-War Cay to see local craftsmen build the Abaco Dinghy as they had for five generations; Great Guana Cay to greet the dolphins Bahama Mama and Princess along with the activities of sailing, windsurfing, swimming, pedal boating, snorkeling, tubing and more. This location had the Bahamas barbecue and live music.

The final stop was Treasure Cay for a round of golf or sets of tennis at a nominal additional fee. After dinner, Captain Hook and Mr. Smee appear to induct guests into their pirate crew for a "Buccaneer Bash" that includes fire-eaters, limbo dancer and Junkanoo musicians. This is all followed by a special midnight buffet on the beach.

The Big Red Boat promoted that it offered "Cruisine", the finest in cruise cuisine with all fruits, vegetables and produce market-fresh and all breads and pastries homemade daily. There were both elegant and casual dining options and all food was inclusive in the price for the cruise. Each night was a themed dinner: French Night, Italian Night, America the Beautiful Night and Caribbean Night.

Special low-fat, low-cholesterol entrees were available as was a special children's menu. Every night was a Midnight Buffet with delicacies from around the world. Besides the usual chocolate mints on the pillow each night, kids were given a bag of The Big Red Boat's exclusive "Chocolate Ship Cookies".

Night time entertainment included shows by the Las Vegas *Legends in Concert* show with performers impersonating Dolly Parton, Elvis Presley, Tina Turner and more as well as the standard comedians and magicians.

By 1991, the cruise line had won the *Grand Prix Mondial du Voyage* for five consecutive years with the World Travel Award Committee naming it the Cruise Line of the Year for excellence in shipboard service and innovative family programs. The youth counselors earned the *On Board Service Award* for providing outstanding activities and services for every kid on board.

For a three day cruise, the *Oceanic* would depart every Friday from Port Canaveral at 4:30pm and return to port Monday at 9:00am. For a four day cruise, it departed Monday at 4:30pm and returned Friday at 8:00am. It was staffed by a crew of 530 and its cruise speed was roughly 27 knots.

According to cabin selection and season, there were nine pricing tiers per person based on double occupancy ranging from roughly $700 to $1,400 for the seven days. Super Value off season was less and Premier offered the three and four day cruises without adding the WDW part of the vacation package at less as well as offering the option to add additional days to the hotel and theme parks.

The Big Red Boat included the upper Sun Deck (with jogging track), Pool Deck, Premier Deck (with Pluto's Playhouse and children recreation center), Lounge Deck (with the Lucky Star Casino with slot machines, the Broadway Showroom, the Starlight Cabaret, Milky Way Shops, Astro Meeting Room), Continental Deck (with Beauty Salon and Massage Room), Restaurant Deck (Seven Continents Restaurant, Ship's Infirmary), Atlantic Deck, and Bahamas Deck (Hollywood Theater).

As described in its marketing:

> The Big Red Boat is America's premier family vacation but it's also one of America's best Honeymoon values, and a great place for singles to meet new friends.
>
> A cruise aboard The Big Red Boat isn't for families only. Kids have their own activities and play centers so you have plenty of time to relax and enjoy. We also offer packages for a family reunion vacation.
>
> With The Big Red Boat, the way you spend your vacation is up to you!

Many of these aspects were later incorporated into the Disney Cruise Line approach to cruising.

The Birth of DCL

Just as Disney revolutionized the concepts of animation and the amusement park, Disney also reinvented the cruise ship experience with rotating dining each evening to different restaurants but with the same servers, an extensively dedicated area for children, its own cruise terminal as well as having its own private island in the Bahamas among many other things.

CEO Michael Eisner saw that there was a boom in the cruise ship business in the 1990s and that Disney could transform that experience as part of his plan for a "Disney Decade" that would expand the Walt Disney Company into other business areas.

In so doing, Disney could keep all the money "in house" rather than sharing it with an outside cruise line partner. The initial goal was to have Walt Disney World visitors extend their vacations by combining a resort stay with a short cruise.

Just as Eisner envisioned Pleasure Island overshadowing Church Street Station, Disney Animal Kingdom trouncing Busch Gardens, Disney MGM Studios undercutting Universal Studios Orlando and Typhoon Lagoon stealing guests who were going to Wet'n'Wild, Eisner felt that a Disney Cruise Line could corner the family market for cruises from any competitor.

Officially, much of the credit for the Disney Cruise Line belongs to then Executive Vice President and Chief Strategic Officer of the Walt Disney Company, Lawrence P. Murphy, whose role was to guide the Walt Disney Company's expansion into new business arenas.

Eisner told author John Heminway that he was bothered by the appearance of modern cruise ships because they didn't capture the sense of romance that had been inherent in the classic experience that had been depicted so well in many of the films of the 1930s and 1940s.

Eisner recalled:

> (The modern ships) didn't look like ships to me. Hotels, yes. All glass and see-through elevators. Those ships were more about Vegas than about the sea. I know they are hugely popular and I could see why people loved going on them, but it simply wasn't for me. Every fiber in my body revolted against building such a ship.
>
> There was another concern I had at the time about forming a partnership with an existing cruise line. We at Disney overspend

on "guest experience." We deliver to our guests more than they expect. I didn't believe a partner—any partner—would understand. They would consider our spending over the top.

I wanted our ship to bring back a feeling of the great times. I can remember seeing my grandparents off on the *Queen Mary* to Europe. I went down to the dock and I can recall the bustle, vast steamer trunks carried aboard.

Later, I was on the last voyage of the *Mauretania*. It was enormous fun. That image of the classic ship and the great ocean passage has stayed with me. It is the romance I feel people are seeking.

Judson Green, former president of Walt Disney Attractions, told writer Heminway:

We woke up and realized we knew how to cruise from a functional point of view in respect to hotel, food and beverage, merchandise, entertainment and world wide sales.

If you think about all the disciplines reflected onboard a ship, we had them all except one... the ability to 'drive the ship'... and that we could acquire. Our core competency is guest satisfaction. It's something we realized could easily be transferred to the high seas.

Basically, the Disney Company had three options: partner with a distinguished existing cruise line, steer clear of the cruise line business completely or have Disney form a cruise line of its own. The final decision after an impassioned presentation by Murphy was to go into the cruise line business at a substantial financial investment and be distinctly Disney.

The Disney executives were completely innocent about cruising. Some had gone on a cruise or two and Wing Chao, executive vice president of Master Planning for Imagineering, admitted that his knowledge was based on two short cruise vacations he had taken, as well as watching *The Love Boat* television show on a regular basis.

Architect Mike Reinnger who was Vice President Product Development and had worked with architects Michael Graves and Robert Stern on Disney resort hotels had been on one unmemorable Caribbean cruise he and his wife had won as a door prize at an event. He was assigned the task of gathering knowledge about ship building.

Chao remembered:

After Michael and Frank decided to get into the cruise business, Michael basically said, 'We want the best naval architects to design the ship to create the most magical floating resort'. Joe Wood, Chris Crary and I investigated and identified thereof the most talented naval architects in Europe.

After the first round of interviews, we floated the idea to them that we wanted a design competition, a process that we've used before with some of our hotel designs. Michael said, 'A Disney ship should be unique, different from any other ship floating today'.

Michael challenged us to "design a ship that would capture the classic elegance of the legendary ocean liners but the ship should also look modern with all the latest technologies aboard."

Designs flowed in, including a re-imagined version of Captain Nemo's submarine from the film *20,000 Leagues Under the Sea*, one that resembled a floating citrus plantation grown in an aquarium with a row of leaping cartoon fish painted along the hull, another than used the ship's funnel as a version of the Magic Kingdom centerpiece, one where the ship's profile was like a floating swan, and one called *Disney Fantasia* that looked like a massive futuristic, sleek, silver spacecraft.

Eisner told the three final architects in contention that "I want you to out-tradition tradition. Go home and make a modern classic."

Those three architect firms were Robert Tillberg of Viken, Sweden, Njal Eide from Oslo, Norway and also from Oslo the partnership of Peter Yran and Bjorn Storbaaten. They were invited to tour Walt Disney World and observe hotels, restaurants and attractions to see how Disney committed to craftsmanship, theming, guest service and attention to detail.

Surprisingly, it was Eide who had expressed that he did not care to design "nostalgic" ships who was the one who came up with a design that had the hallmarks of the great traditional ships of the past but with a contemporary feel. He included two funnels in his design, even though modern ships only needed one and that one is often concealed. The stacks were purposefully angled to give an aerodynamic look as well as separating the three pool areas.

In the classic ships of the past, lifeboats were placed high at the top. For safety reasons, lifeboats are now located at the promenade deck. To solve that design issue, Eide recalls, "How could I create that classic look within the letter of the law? I, therefore, chose to place huge bay windows on those top decks and I divided those windows into modules, each about 12 meters long, cantilevered, each suggesting life boats when viewed at a distance."

When they saw the model, the other two competitors agreed that Eide had captured the core of what Disney wanted. It captured the glamour and style of the classic ships of the past but was clearly a modern interpretation with contemporary features.

Project manager Kevin Cummings remembered:

> The challenge was to parlay our Disney design mentality and culture into building something extraordinary and one-of-a-kind, down to the smallest detail.

The 875 staterooms were made twenty-five percent larger than those on other cruise ships with seventy-three percent outside staterooms (forty-four with verandahs while the others had larger than usual portholes). The staterooms had more storage space and many had two bathrooms.

Ralph Ireland, assistant development manager on the *Disney Magic*, said:

> We had one of the best furniture makers in the world, Molteni and C in Italy, for the staterooms. They brought over their best craftsmen to work on the suites. The one thing that makes me happier than anything else is to hear people talking about the staterooms and how great they are. A lot of travel agents on a pre-christening cruise couldn't believe how much better the quality is.

Challenges faced by the Imagineers including finding materials to conform to heightened fire regulations as well as taking into consideration the fact that all systems and services would have to be contained within the ship's deck and be as eco-sensitive as possible. Not to mention having to constantly check on product quality during construction to make sure that design elements were not suffering from foreign-language translation issues.

At the same time, in WDI's facility in Tujunga, California, durability tests were being conducted. Project engineer Eric Merz recalled:

> The items we built for the cruise line needed to be able to survive a harsh marine environment including high winds, corrosion and the listing and tilting of the ship itself. The paint finish needed to be able to withstand years, not months, at sea.

Technical director for show production John Nelson added:

> We elected to use an automotive paint finish tested at a facility that used an accelerating chamber to analyze degradation of the paint.

In addition, all the elements from props, murals, fixtures and sculptures that were produced at the Tujunga location had to be transported to Italy for installation on the ship.

The Mickey Pool slide was eighteen feet wide. The crate was so big that it couldn't be trucked during normal operating hours because it required special permits.

The solution was to have the trucking company show up at the facility at four o'clock in the morning to begin loading but clearances to drive it on service streets to the Long Beach Harbor were not approved until three o'clock the next morning. When it finally arrived at the harbor, it was too large to fit in the cargo hold so it had to be strapped to the deck for its voyage to Italy.

Dr. Hartmut Essliner of "frogdesign" who had been brought in to tweak the design said:

> An object this large—a ship—should be like a person you want to be with. It should have human qualities. The more an object responds to the body, the more we like it. The bridge and the ship should harken you to move on into a new world. Such a feel is badly missing on most cruise ships today.

Disney approached the design based on the age group that would utilize a particular space. Project Coordinator Paolo Simoniti marveled, "Other ships have only fifth the space dedicated to children as does Disney and including having rounded corners."

Eisner was extremely hands-on going to a minimum of five different meetings for every room on the ship:

> I went to see life-size mock-ups of the ship's staterooms in Italy before we committed to any design detail. We change everything three to four times at least.

The United States no longer had a shipyard that could build such a ship although such places did still exist in Japan, Finland, Germany and Italy. On May 20, 1995 the Fincantieri Shipyards in Italy with over two hundred years experience in building ships was awarded the contract. The shipyard aggressively sought the contract because having a relationship with Disney was a matter of enormous prestige.

The ship had to be comfortable for passengers while sailing at 21 knots, "supremely seaworthy" and other requirements that surpassed all current quality standards as well as being capable of going through the Panama Canal which determined its maximum length.

Because of the shipyard capacity and a tight schedule to get the work done, it was decided to build the ship in two parts. The bow was done in the Ancona shipyard and the stern in the shipyard one hundred miles to the north in Marghera (just outside Venice). Joining the two parts together was technologically possible but it had never ever been done before in the cruise ship industry and is a process called Jumboisation.

Coordinating construction between both Fincantieri yards so that the hulls would be ready at the same time and match once they were brought together was a challenge. Another challenge was one frustrating delay after another because of different cultural attitudes.

President of Imagineering Ken Wong stated:

> With a ship, you place an order. You do not have control of the process, the way we control everything down to the tiniest detail in the construction process of, say, Disney's Animal Kingdom.
>
> You can have review and acceptance approval at the very end, but along the way, the shipyard is in charge. Instead of driving the car, you're in the back seat. They may listen to you—and they may not.

The Italian attitude was to have no sense of urgency. They did not work on holidays or have a firm schedule. In fact, they did not have tools to track the schedule.

Finally Wong took a team to Italy for four months to try to address the challenges. The team was compromised of senior vice president of Worldwide Production Matthew Priddy (to diagnose problems in technical matters), vice president of Human Resources Ronni Fridman and vice president of Facilities Engineering at Disneyland T. Irby.

The bow was pulled out to sea by ocean going tugboats at a speed of three knots for over forty-two hours. In mid–April 1997, the two sections were put together during a four day process where a series of match points with interlocking plates were joined with a variance of never more than one millimeter. Most other ships have overlapping sheets but the *Disney Magic* was joined edge-to-edge for a seamless outer hull surface.

It was completed by Friday, April 18, 1997 with additions over the next few weeks including craning one of the funnels into place and installing the communication mast.

The two separate sections from Fincantieri Maghera Shipyard (for the stern) and the Fincantieri Ancona Shipyard (for the bow) were joined approximately where the entrance of Lumiere's restaurant is located. Since the two parts had to be brought together, the forward half of the ship technically has put in more miles at sea than the aft section.

On May 13, 1997 at 10:30am, the complete ship floated for the first time and shortly after noon, blasts of horns, the flight of fifty doves, salutes from Mickey, Minnie, Donald and Goofy, spirited cheers from the press, shipyard workers and other onlookers as well as the obligatory speeches signaled that the *Disney Magic* was now docked at a quay in deep water.

This event was followed by several sea trials pushing the ship to its limits to check things that could only be examined under operating conditions. After passing all tests with flying colors, the remaining interior spaces were finished.

Ownership was transferred from the shipyard to Disney and the vessel headed out to sea for its transatlantic crossing from Venice to its new homeport at Port Canaveral in Florida on July 1, 1998. It arrived July 15.

Priddy pointed out:

> The ship is a miniature destination resort in itself: a hotel; a retail, dining and entertainment complex; aspects of "E-ticket" experiences. Almost nothing exists that isn't already in existence at Disney except that you've got it all on a platform moving on the sea.

Disney commissioned the *Disney Magic* to be "purpose built" from the keel up to capture the Golden Era of Ocean Cruising as well as a family-friendly atmosphere and where operational areas were kept hidden from the guests.

Of course, at the time, the ship was not initially named during construction which was the standard tradition. Eisner wanted the *Disney Magic* (then only known by its block number "5989") to be named after Walt Disney. However, when that suggestion was rejected, Eisner reportedly told his executives that if it couldn't be named after Walt then it needed to be named after what Walt had created: Magic.

The *Disney Magic* harks back to the era of classic great ships when they were reflections of that time's best architects, artists, designers and artisans. It truly evokes the glamour of the Golden

Age with its beautiful Art Deco design as well as its sense of Disney whimsy blended with a nautical theme.

Architect Mike Reininger, who was hired as vice president of Production Development, said:

> I see the interior of the ship as an emotional storyline.
>
> It must be approached not just as an 'interior' but as a stage set. Our guests will walk onboard and then pass through spaces, from one story to another, all using a similar vocabulary that integrates them to the sea, legendary ocean liners and Disney. We intend the story to have impact at every level. For that to occur, we have adopted a central vision.

How many guests notice subtle details such as the shower curtain having the faint imprint of a ship's mooring rope that occasionally twists into the silhouette of Mickey Mouse's head?

Director of design and development Bob Holland said:

> When the ship was sitting dead in the water, tied to the pier, it was very static. But when you put the ship in motion, it has a grace, spirit and life of its own that is much more intense and unlike anything I've been involved with in constructing a building.

Ken Wong said:

> People are touched by this ship. In a speech I made when the ship was celebrated as being complete, I said, "We dreamed of a ship that, just by looking at her, would make you smile." This definitely makes you smile.
>
> It was the most grueling, terrifying, rewarding, and ultimately proud experience we've ever had. It was Imagineering at its absolute best which I'd sum up in three words: great hard work.

DCL became the dawn of a new innovative vacation experience. Its sister ship, the *Disney Wonder* was completed the next year so that there would always be a DCL ship at sea.

The Disney Cruise Fleet

Disney Cruise Line is a subsidiary of Walt Disney World, originally incorporated in 1996 as Magical Cruise Company Limited, headquartered in Celebration, Florida. The current CEO since October 2017 is Anthony Connelly. The ships are officially registered in the Bahamas for legal reasons.

The difference between a boat and a ship is basically the size. You can put a boat on a ship but you can't put a ship on a boat.

The Disney Cruise Line has four ships: *Disney Magic*, *Disney Wonder*, *Disney Dream* and *Disney Fantasy*. Three more ships will be added to the fleet each year starting in 2021. Unlike some other cruise ships, there are no gambling casinos. All the ships have stabilizers which are horizontal, submerged flaps that can be extended from the vessels to help minimize rolling motion.

The *Disney Magic* and *Disney Wonder* are considered "Magic Class or Classic". The *Disney Dream* and *Disney Fantasy* are considered "Dream Class". The three new ships will be considered "Triton Class".

In 2019 nearly twenty-five million people decided to take a cruise according to *Cruise Market Watch*. Nearly forty percent of those cruisers were people who had been on at least one previous cruise. Of those, a mere two percent travelled solo while the others usually brought a significant other, a family or were part of a larger group.

The Caribbean is the most popular cruise destination accounting for a little over thirty-seven percent of bookings. While DCL offers other itineraries including Alaskan, Bermudan, Canadian, European, Panama Canal and Transaltantic cruises, the majority of its business are the different Bahamian and Caribbean cruises from Port Canaveral and Miami.

In 2019, the Disney Cruise Line earned a guest satisfaction score of 871 compared to the overall survey average of 824 according to J.D. Power Satisfaction Report. *U.S. News*

& *World Report* awarded it Best Cruise Line for Families and Best Cruise Line in the Caribbean.

The DCL has won over 250 other such awards from travel and general media sources including recognition for hospitality, dining, family and entertainment for every year since it first launched and received the Cacique Award (Bahamas) as "Cruise Line of the Year" in 1999.

DCL receives consistently high ratings across all categories. Its main competitor is Royal Caribbean International which some people prefer in certain offerings especially price considerations for similar itineraries.

Imagineering Senior Development Manager Lysa Migliorati said:

> We pay careful attention to detail and demand a high quality of design and materials," said. "We look carefully at the transition spaces that connect the various venues and create a cohesive relationship of the designs. We take pride in hiring the best interior design firms around the world to help us create successful spaces for all our guests.

Imagineer Joe Lanzisero stated:

> One of our challenges is to balance the amount of, I'm going to say, 'Disney whimsy' with elegance.

Greg Butkus, a concept designer for Walt Disney Imagineering said:

> [The goal was to make] the storytelling on the ship unique and different from the parks. Ultimately, we wanted to create a one-of-a-kind Disney experience. I always wondered what Walt would ever have thought about a theme park on a ship. I believe Walt would be quite pleased.

This book concentrates on the storytelling of the DCL. For more information on the mechanics of cruising on the DCL like pricing, itineraries, amenities and other similar tips, I recommend the most current copy of *The Unofficial Guide Disney Cruise Line*. In addition, Scott Sanders' Disney Cruise Line Blog (www.disneycruiselineblog.com) is extremely helpful as are various other websites including www.DCLNews.com and the Disney Parks Blog www.disneyparks.disney.go.com/blog which features news of changes.

High Seas Glossary

Art Deco: An art style characterized by slender forms, straight lines, geometric designs and bold, solid colors with a sleekness often expressive of modern technology. The style of the interior used on the *Disney Magic* and the *Disney Dream*.

Art Nouveau: An art style that includes whimsical swirling, curving wave designs and uses an organic "art from nature" feel. The style of interior used on the *Disney Wonder* and the *Disney Fantasy*.

Aft: The back area of the ship. On the DCL ships the area where the primary food locations are generally located. The term comes from the word "after", basically the section after the main part of the ship.

Bow: The very front of the outside of the ship pronounced like "bough". On DCL, the art on the bow includes Sorcerer Mickey (*Disney Magic*), Steamboat Willie (*Disney Wonder*), Captain Mickey (*Disney Dream*), and Sorcerer Mickey (*Disney Fantasy*).

Bridge: The location where the captain and the crew navigate the ship.

DCL: Disney Cruise Line

Deck: The floor stretching across a level of the ship.

Forward: The front area of a ship. On the DCL ships the area where the entertainment theaters are generally located.

Funnel: Traditionally the large hollow tube through which exhaust from the ship's engine can escape. Modern ships only require one. On the DCL ships, one of its two funnels is used as an entertainment venue.

Galley: The name for a kitchen on a ship.

Gangway: The location on the side of a ship where passengers and crew can board and disembark.

Hull: The name for the outer frame of the ship's body.

Knot: A unit of speed equal to one nautical mile per hour (roughly 1.15 miles an hour). On average, the DCL ships cruise at 24 to 25 miles per hour. The term came from counting the number of spaced knots in the rope line that unspooled from the reel on a ship during a specific time period.

Maritime: Related to the sea, in particular shipping.

Midship: The middle area of the ship. On the DCL ships, this is the entrance area with the multi-deck atrium.

Nautical: Pertaining to the ocean, in particular sailors, shipping and navigation.

Port: The term for the left-hand side of the ship when facing forward. In addition, it can also refer to the city or harbor venue where the ship docks like Port Canaveral.

Porthole: The name of the circular windows on the side of the ship.

Stateroom: The name for the rooms on the ship and also referred to as "cabin" on other cruise lines.

Stern: The very back of the exterior of the ship. On the DCL ships, three-dimensional figures of Disney characters hang off the back of each ship trying to finish painting the name of the ship: Goofy (*Disney Magic*), Donald Duck and Huey (*Disney Wonder*), Sorcerer Mickey and two Fantasia brooms (*Disney Dream*), Dumbo and Timothy the Mouse (*Disney Fantasy*).

Starboard: The term for the right-hand side of the ship when facing forward.

Tender: A small boat that transfers passengers from the ship to land when the port waters are too shallow to allow the ship to dock next to a pier.

Additional Location Directions: If your stateroom has a fish on the outside of the door, then you are on the port (left) side since it has the same number of letters as "fish," and if you are on the starboard (right) side, your stateroom has a seahorse outside the door because it is the roughly the same number of letters and begins with the letter "s".

To tell whether you are forward or aft on the *Disney Dream* or *Disney Fantasy*, look at the design of a ship's wheel encompassing a map on the carpet in the hallway. If it is upright, then you are heading forward. If it is upside down, you are heading aft. The nautical signal flags that decorate the design spell out the name of the ship. The top point of the stars above and below the design all point forward.

Each deck is the length of three football fields so it is important to know locations to avoid excess walking. State room numbers are the deck number, followed by a three-digit number.

Staterooms x000 through x499 (where x is the deck number) are on the port side of the ship, while staterooms x500 through x999 are on the starboard side of the ship.

Disney Magic

Maiden Voyage: July 30, 1998

- Passenger Capacity Maximum: 2,713
- Crew: 950
- Total Staterooms: 877
- Gross Tonnage: 84,000 tons
- Length: 964 feet originally (In 2014, twenty feet of steel were added to the back of the ship to support new additions made to the ship including the AquaDunk.)
- Beam (widest portion of the ship): 106 feet
- Shipyard: Fincantieri—Marghera & Ancona, Italy
- Cruising Speed: 21.5 knots

Godmother: Patricia "Patty" Ann Dailey Disney (1935 - 2012), the wife of Roy E. Disney at the time of the ship's christening on July 28, 1998. They had four children and seventeen grandchildren. They were divorced in 2007 after almost 52 years of marriage. She was known for her outgoing nature and her philanthropy including the Roy and Patricia Disney Family Foundation and the Roy and Patricia Disney Family Cancer Center.

A ship's Godmother christens the ship and blesses it. She is entrusted with guiding this ship to and around all its destinations by placing a blessing upon it. Roy, the son of Walt Disney's older brother Roy Oliver Disney, was named the ship's Godfather at the same time.

In October 1998, he received the Disney Legends award. He held several sailing speed records and in 2008 married Leslie DeMeuse, a producer he had worked with on several sailing documentaries.

Atrium Statue: Helmsman Mickey
The bronze statue of Mickey Mouse wearing an oilskin slicker, a waterproof garment worn by fishermen in wet weather, and straining at a steering wheel as if during a storm, was designed by Imagineer John Hench.

It was inspired by Leonard Craske's famous eight-foot tall 1923 (the year the Disney Studios started) statue, "Man At The Wheel," showcased at the Fisherman's Memorial in Gloucester, Massachusetts. "Mickey at the Wheel" was sculpted by Valerie Edwards, a protégé of Blaine Gibson.

Like the original, the atrium statue serves as a monument to the bravery and dedication of sailors everywhere. There is an exact copy of the statue at Tokyo DisneySea in Japan.

DCL commissioned a limited edition serigraph of 8,500 copies Helmsman Mickey measuring fourteen inches by fourteen inches in a frame in 1998 to commemorate the launch of the ship. Walt Disney Art Classics was the publisher of this edition. Disney artists created the master for this image, which was used by Team Art Studios in Gardena, Ca to produce this print. The silk screens used to create the edition are destroyed when the edition was complete and the orginal artwork is archived with Walt Disney Art Classics.

Bow Art: Sorcerer Mickey

Aft Statue: A fifteen foot high fiberglass Goofy with paint brushes appearing to finish painting the letters of the ship's name. Goofy is depicted as a boatswain (or "bosun") in charge of the hull. The figure was designed by John Hench.

Art Style: Art Deco

Restaurants:
- Rapunzel's Royal Table (recreating the ballroom of the royal castle during a celebration of Rapunzel's birthday)
- Lumiere's (recreating the interior of the Beast's castle from *Beauty and the Beast*)
- Animator's Palate (recreating the interior of a Disney animation studio including elements from Pixar)
- Cabanas (a buffet style restaurant meant to suggest "where everyday is a picnic on the beach" and a reference to the tent-like temporary structure often found on a beach)
- Palo (recreating an upscale restaurant in Venice, Italy as an homage to the birthplace of the first two DCL ships)

Nightclubs and Lounges: Cove Café, Fathoms, Keys, D Lounge, Promenade Lounge, O'Gills Pub, Signals.

Quick Serve: Duck In Diner, Pinocchio's Pizzeria, Frozone Treats.

Entertainment Shows:
- *Twice Charmed: An Original Twist on the Cinderella Story* (The evil stepmother and stepsisters go back in time thanks to an evil fairy godfather to destroy the second glass slipper that Cinderella produced for the prince so she could live happily ever after.)
- *Tangled: The Musical* (An adaptation of the animated feature. Animated feature film *Tangled* composer Alan Menken created three new songs specifically for this production with lyricist Glenn Slater.)
- *Disney Dreams: An Enchanted Classic* (Peter Pan must help a young girl named Anne Marie find her own magic before sunrise by taking her through moments from several classic animated features.)

Disney Wonder

Maiden Voyage: August 15, 1999
- Passenger Capacity Maximum: 2,713
- Crew: 950
- Staterooms: 877
- Gross Tonnage: 84,000 tons
- Length: 964 feet
- Beam (the widest portion of the ship): 106 feet
- Shipyard: Fincantieri—Marghera, Italy
- Cruising Speed: 21.5 knots

Godmother: Tinker Bell (the first time an animated or fictional character has been the Godmother of a ship). The *Disney Wonder* was the first ship to ever be christened at night so they could project with lasers Tinker Bell flying along the side of the ship and sprinkling pixie dust. It was followed by fireworks.

President of Disney Attractions Paul Pressler said at the christening on October 1, 1999:

> The christening of a new ship is steeped in tradition and we at the Walt Disney Company are pleased to continue that tradition this evening.
>
> A woman of high character and accomplishments is chosen to be the godmother of the ship and ensures good fortune for the ship, her captain and the passengers and crew.

Legends are hard to come by but we believe we have chosen the perfect godmother to christen the *Disney Wonder*. She truly is a Disney Legend. She worked at Walt Disney's side almost from the very beginning.

As he created the magic, she was there, always there, to make it happen. He counted on her for her unique creative talent and she never let him down. They had a very special relationship and over the years, she has continued to make the magic happen.

Her unique talents, her bright personality, her boundless energy bring happiness to all of us. I think you know her very well and now the moment has come to introduce this very special lady. Mickey, would you do the honors?

A costumed Mickey pointed to a large screen where "a maker of magic, a lovable luminary" appeared in the dark sky with clouds, Tinker Bell. The screen went dark and her laser-projected image appeared on the side of the ship.

Atrium Statue: Ariel Sitting Pretty. Supposedly, she is sitting underwater which is why her hair swirls upwards.

Bow Art: Steamboat Willie

Aft Statue: Donald Duck hanging by ropes desperately trying to finish up the lettering paint job on the stern while up above his nephew Huey with a pair of scissors is threatening to cut the ropes.

Art Style: Art Nouveau

Restaurants:
- Triton's (recreating the palace of the father of The Little Mermaid)
- Tiana's Place (recreating the New Orleans restaurant from the animated feature *The Princess and the The Frog*)
- Animators Palate (recreating a Disney animation studio with elements from Pixar)
- Palo (recreating an upscale restaurant in Venice, Italy as an homage to where the first two DCL ships were built)
- Cabanas (a buffet style restaurant meant to suggest "where everyday is a picnic on the beach" and a reference to the tent-like temporary structure often found on a beach)

Nighclubs and Lounges: Crown & Fin Pub, Cove Café, Cadillac Lounge, Azure, D Lounge, Promenade Lounge, Signals.

Quick Serve: Daisy De-Lites, Pete's Boiler Bites, Pinocchio's Pizzeria.

Entertainment Shows:
- *The Golden Mickeys* (Meant to mimic award shows like the Oscars ceremony but there is no competition involved and it is just an excuse to showcase musical highlights from some Disney animated features. A subplot involves the shy stage manager named Ensign Bensen becoming the host and blossoming into a confident person.)
- *Frozen: A Musical Spectacular* (An elaborate adaptation of the animated feature that includes some puppets of Sven and Olaf by Michael Curry, responsible for the puppets in the Broadway show *The Lion King*.)
- *Disney Dreams: An Enchanted Classic* (Peter Pan must help a young girl named Anne Marie find her own magic before sunrise by taking her through moments in several classic animated features.)

Disney Dream

Maiden Voyage: January 26, 2011
- Passenger Capacity Maximum: 4,000
- Crew: 1, 458
- Staterooms: 1,250
- Gross Tonnage: 130,000 tons
- Length: 1,115 feet
- Beam (widest portion of the ship): 121 feet
- Shipyard: Meyer Werft—Papenburg, Germany
- Cruising Speed: 22 knots

Godmother: Jennifer Hudson

Disney president and CEO Bob Iger and actress/singer Jennifer Hudson were on hand to christen the Disney Dream on January 19, 2011. Hudson began her career as a singing performer on the *Disney Wonder* back in 2003, which is the reason given for her selection. She won a Best Supporting Academy Award for her role in the movie *Dreamgirls* (2006).

Hudson said:

> I was on a Disney cruise line the year I decided to audition for *American Idol*. I was Calliope the muse in *Hercules: The Muse-ical* and I was also the *Circle of Life* soloist in a Disney's cruise show. And in that show, I narrated the show, I did a lot of singing and we had a lot of choreography, as well. It's part of how I got *Dreamgirls* because they took that as an acting credit.

For the christening she sang *Who Knows Where a Dream Might Lead* from the DCL show *The Golden Mickeys* because she played the role of Rona Rivers in that show that originated on the *Disney Wonder* in 2003.

The ceremony was a bit unusual in that Hudson did not physically smash a bottle of champagne across the hull, but a helicopter appeared and hoisted a 16-foot-tall champagne-shaped bottle high in the air. The bottle, according to the Disney press release was filled "with dreams of adventure, fantasy, friendship, romance and fun".

Hudson lifted a magic wand high in the air that began to spark as she asked God "to bless the ship and all who would sail on her" as the huge bottle smashed on the forward bow, unleashing fireworks from the ship.

Atrium Statue: Admiral Donald Duck

The five-foot tall bronze Admiral Donald Duck statue on a marble pedestal in the atrium lobby was inspired by the animated short *Sea Scouts* (1939), where Donald Duck is similarly attired. The crew will tell you that it had to be "Admiral" Donald Duck, because he insisted on a higher ranking than "Captain" Mickey Mouse.

Bow Art: Captain Mickey

Aft Statue: Sorcerer Mickey leisurely directing two of the anthropomorphic brooms from *Fantasia* (1940) to finish painting the name of the ship

The Sorcerer Mickey Mouse on the stern is about fourteen feet long. It was constructed out of stainless steel and fiberglass and weighs approximately 2,500 pounds.

It was sculpted at Walt Disney Imagineering in California, structurally designed by engineers at Disney Cruise Line and Meyer Werft in Germany, manufactured in Sarasota, Florida, finish-painted in Orlando, and then transported by ship to Germany for final installation on the *Disney Dream*. From sculpture to the stern of the Disney Dream was a journey of about 15,000 miles for Mickey Mouse.

Art Style: Art Deco

Restaurants:

- Enchanted Garden (inspired by the fabled elaborate gardens of Versailles in France)
- Royal Palace (recreating the ballroom from *Beauty and the Beast* with elements from *Cinderella*)
- Animators Palate (recreating a Disney animation studio)
- Palo (recreating an upscale restaurant in Venice, Italy as an homage to where the first two DCL ships were built)
- Remy (inspired by the French restaurant in the Pixar movie *Ratatouille*)
- Cabanas (a buffet style restaurant meant to suggest "where everyday is a picnic on the beach" and a reference to the tent-like temporary structure often found on a beach)

Nightclubs and Lounges: Currents, Skyline, Cove Café, District Lounge, Pink: Wine & Champagne Bar, D Lounge, Evolution, Vista Café, Pub 687, Meridian, Bon Voyage.

Quick Serve: Themed after Pixar animated feature *Cars*, Flo's V8 Café Food Court includes Luigi's Pizza, Tow Mater Grill, and Fillmore's Favorites stations that serve hamburgers, sandwiches, pizza, fruit and more. Eye Scream (based on the one-eyed Mike Wazowski from *Monsters Inc*.) serves ice cream and Frozone Treats (based on the superhero from *The Incredibles*) has fruit smoothies.

Vanellope's Sweets and Treats has a selection of bulk candy, pre-packaged Disney candy, macaroons cookies, character apples, fudge, rice crispy treats, cupcakes and other tasty treats, as well as a selection of ice cream, frozen yogurt, and gelato with selections varying each day of the cruise. Shop is inspired by the Pixar animated feature *Wreck-It Ralph*.

Entertainment Shows:

- *The Golden Mickeys: A Timeless Tribute* (Meant to mimic award shows like the Oscars ceremony but there is no competition involved and it is just an excuse to showcase

highlights from some Disney animated features. A subplot involves the shy stage manager named Ensign Bensen becoming the host and blossoming into a confident person.)
- *Beauty and the Beast* (An adaptation inspired by the 2017 live action remake of the 1991 animated feature.)
- *Disney's Believe* (A distracted botanist father who doesn't believe in magic is guided by the genie from *Aladdin* to help reconnect with his young daughter on her birthday.)

Disney Fantasy

Maiden Voyage: March 31, 2012
- Passenger Capacity: 4,000
- Crew: 1,458
- Staterooms: 1,250
- Gross Tonnage: 130,000 tons
- Length: 1,115 feet
- Beam (widest portion of the ship): 121 feet
- Shipyard: Meyer Werft—Papenburg, Germany
- Cruising Speed: 22 knots

Godmother: Mariah Carey
Carey was selected because of her multi-award winning song *Fantasy* (1995) that became the second song in Billboard history, and the first by a female, to debut atop the *Billboard Hot 100*. She had performed at the Disney Parks Christmas Day Parade in both 2005 and 2010.

The christening took place March 1, 2012 in New York. Carey did the christening announcement in the atrium lobby of the ship accompanied by Disney CEO Bob Iger and Parks and Resorts Chairman Tom Staggs.

A larger-than-life faux champagne bottle spouted glitter while Carey's husband Nick Cannon accompanied Minnie Mouse, who actually struck the hull of the *Fantasy* with a real bottle of champagne to bring the line's fourth ship into service.

Atrium Statue: Mademoiselle Minnie
Dressed in vintage fashion of the 1930s and posing with a closed parasol and a round hat box at her feet (not the "steamer luggage" usually cited in most descriptions that implies a trunk), the

bronze sculpture is meant to be reminiscent of travelers during the height of transatlantic cruise crossings going from New York to France (which is why she is a "mademoiselle").

Bruce Vaughn, chief creative executive for Walt Disney Imagineering, said:

> The 1930s time of travel was the most romantic, so that is where we started with our design. We want our guests to get excited just seeing the ship—evoking a beautiful, classic 1930s ocean liner. At our heart, we are storytellers. We take families on vacation and immerse them in stories. We want to transport them out of everyday reality to a different reality.

Bow Art: Sorcerer Mickey

Aft Statue: Timothy Mouse and Dumbo
The characters combined weigh more than 2,300 pounds. Dumbo is a little more than eight feet long from head to tail with an "ear span" of seven feet. Timothy sits 2'6" tall on Dumbo's hat and is holding a paint brush that's about 3'10" long. Dumbo was sculpted from large foam blocks by Walt Disney Imagineering artists in Glendale, California. The sculpted pieces were then shipped to Florida where Disney craftsmen and artists created him in fiberglass and paint over a frame of marine-grade stainless steel. They were installed in Papenburg, Germany.

Art Style: Art Nouveau

Restaurants:
- Enchanted Garden (inspired by the fabled elaborate gardens of Versailles in France)
- Royal Court (recreating the ballroom from *Beauty and the Beast* with elements from *Cinderella*)
- Animators Palate (recreating a Disney animation studio)
- Palo (recreating an upscale restaurant in Venice, Italy as an homage to whtre the first two DCL ships were built)
- Remy (inspired by the French restaurant in the Pixar movie *Ratatouille*)
- Cabanas (a buffet style restaurant meant to suggest "where everyday is a picnic on the beach" and a reference to the tent-like temporary structure often found on a beach)

Nightclubs and Lounges: Currents, Skyline, Cove Café, La Piazza, D Lounge, The Tube, Vista Café, O'Gills Pub, Meridian, Bon Voyage, Ooh La La.

Quick Serve: Themed after Pixar animated feature *Cars*, Flo's V 8 Café Food Court includes Luigi's Pizza, Doc's Grill, and Fillmore's Favorites stations that serve hamburgers, sandwiches, pizza, fruit and more. Eye Scream (based on the one-eyed Mike Wazowski from Monsters Inc.) serves ice cream and Frozone Treats (based on the superhero from The Incredibles) has fruit smoothies.

Sweet On You has a selection of bulk candy, pre-packaged Disney candy, macaroons cookies, character apples, fudge, rice crispy treats, cupcakes and other tasty treats, as well as a selection of ice cream, frozen yogurt, and gelato with selections varying each day of the cruise. Themed after a Mickey and Minnie ice cream parlor from one of their classic short cartoons with full-sized Mickey and Minnie statues sharing a frozen treat at a round table.

Entertainment Shows:

- *Aladdin: A Musical Spectacular* (An adaptation of the animated feature film.)
- *Disney's Believe* (A distracted botanist father who doesn't believe in magic is guided by the genie from *Aladdin* to help reconnect with his young daughter on her birthday.)
- *Frozen: A Musical Spectacular* (An elaborate adaptation of the animated feature that includes some puppets of Sven and Olaf by Michael Curry, responsible for the puppets in the Broadway show *The Lion King*.)

Captain Tom

Tom Forberg was the inaugural captain for all four of the Disney cruise ships, sailing them from Europe to America. He will most probably be the inaugural captain of the upcoming *Disney Wish*.

A veteran who has served on the ships of the long-lost Norwegian American Line, Royal Caribbean and Crystal Cruises, he joined Disney in 1995, three years before the *Disney Magic* set sail on her maiden voyage. When he joined the DCL, it made him the first member of the crew to be hired.

He played a pivotal role in the construction of each of the four Disney Cruise Line ships. Born in Norway, he now has a home in

Treviso, Italy. His wife is Italian so he spends much of his time off the ship there. He also has a place in Orlando, Florida. His mother still lives in Norway as does his brother so he goes to Norway a couple of times a year to visit them.

Forberg, who went to nautical college and Captain's school before becoming a member of the Norwegian Navy, said:

> I started in the [Norwegian] navy. After some time I found out the food was better on the cruise ships, so I left the navy and joined the cruise ships.

Before coming aboard the DCL, Forberg had twenty years of cruise-industry experience, including fifteen of those years as a cruise ship captain.

He continued:

> I had been in the cruise industry for years doing more or less the same thing all the time. So I thought to myself if I join Disney, I'm sure they will have a lot of ideas of how to do cruising in a whole new way. You couldn't really go wrong joining one of the best-known companies in the world.
>
> It's been very rewarding for me as a captain to work for a company like Disney. We do things a little differently, and it's more interesting working for a company like that. It has such a reputation around the world. Everyone has so many nice things to say about Disney.
>
> I still have a lot of fondness for the first two classic ships even though I love the newer ones. It is all about teamwork. Our crew is what really makes the Disney difference.

He was also in command of the *Disney Magic* sailing through the Panama Canal to the West Coast in 2005 and to the Mediterranean in 2007.

In August 2013, Disney Cruise Line executives President Karl Holz, Senior Vice President Anthony Connelly, Captain Mickey and Vice President Bert Swets joined the crew of the *Disney Fantasy* during a ceremony bestowing the honor of the rank of Commodore to Captain Forberg and presented him with a new hat to indicate the change in rank.

Commodore is an honorary term assigned to an officer responsible for commanding multiple ships at one time. Forberg serves as the highest-ranking Disney captain and continues to share the duty of commanding the ships rotationally along with the other captains. The only other cruise line actively using the commodore title is is Cunard with its Commodore Christopher Rynd.

As Forberg said:

> Disney is not a typical cruise line company. It gets so much input from Disney as a mother company that makes cruise business even more interesting. Even if you do the same itinerary, things are still a little bit different.
>
> We see many more families, and how we cater to make sure that each and every family member has the best experience in his or her life is just amazing. Nobody does that better than Disney. And that's a huge difference, how the family as a whole is looked after on a Disney cruise. I personally think it's very nice to have a lot of kids around the ship.
>
> Every year there are a few new technological things coming online. It's just like a car — the basic equipment is more or less the same, but it gets more and more advanced and better and better.
>
> If you looked at the exterior lines of the ship it's reminiscent of the early ocean liners of the '30s, but with modern technology. So if you'd come to the bridge, we have all the state-of-the-art equipment that you'd expect to find on a new ship today, whether it's navigation systems, safety systems and so forth.
>
> We still have a steering wheel but for maneuvering we have a very advanced joystick as well. Incorporated in this joystick you have twin active rudders, five sideways thrusters and the main propulsion. So we can actually move the ship 360 degrees around just moving the joystick. There is a duplicate set-up in the engine room that could control the ship if necessary.
>
> It's like a video game in one way. In fact, we have a simulator for practice. All of the characteristics that we have on the ship are in the simulator and it's probably about 90-percent accurate. So I get a feeling of how our ship will behave already.
>
> Captain Mickey is still the boss. We enjoy having him onboard, and of course the guests like to see him around and also all the other characters.

The Colors of the Ship

Today, cruise line ships are usually painted white with orange-colored lifeboats but the DCL ships have a distinctively different color scheme.

Under the direction of Imagineer John Hench who was senior vice president of Creative Development at the time, colors were selected that would suggest the great transatlantic ocean liners of the Golden Age of Cruising as well as using the colors that are associated with the company icon Mickey Mouse.

The design intent was that the exterior of the ship would suggest the colors of Mickey Mouse: black, white, red (from his pants) and yellow (from his shoes and buttons).

Hench said, "I selected a blue-black because it gives a little more contrast making the white look more brilliant. Using yellow in the white reflects light better. The red-orange stacks are typical though we didn't use a standard color called Cunard red that was named for a competing ship line. We used something similar."

Dr. Harmut Esslinger of "frogdesign" recalled:

> Even though it is the primary color of Mickey Mouse, I think that black is too sinister, too depressing, especially on a Disney ship. We selected a color that was 87 percent black and the rest blue. As a result, that color changes subtly depending upon the time of day, weather and position.

While they were working on the color, a female employee named Monica Gonzalez came into the room wearing dark blue pants. No one had seen that particular color hue before and they used it, calling it "Monica Blue," a tradition that goes back to Disney animation where Tinker Bell's green is called Dreiss Green after an ink and painter who wore that particular color on a dress to work one day.

The ship's twenty bright yellow lifeboats required special permission from the International Maritime Organization to use that color since orange is the standard color because of its high visibility.

Disney was able to demonstrate that the particular yellow color was eleven percent brighter than a red color while being only less than one percent as bright as the orange shade that is the regulation color of the U.S. Coast Guard.

The gold filigree on both the bow and stern to give an added touch of elegance were unique at the time, as well. Only one other liner had sported such a decoration: the *Stella Polaris* built for Norway's Bergen Line in 1927 to carry roughly 165 passengers mostly on North Cape cruises. It was meant to suggest a millionaire-class luxury yacht.

Disney Cruise Terminal

In 1997, the Disney Cruise Terminal at Port Canaveral opened to make the entire DCL story experience more cohesive. The terminal is among the "A" Cruise Terminals, at 9155 Charles M. Rowland Drive in Port Canaveral.

Designed by Acquitectonica and Bruno Elias & Associates and built at a cost of roughly twenty-seven million dollars, it captured the same "classic but modern" theme as the DCL ships with inspiration from classic transit stations in New York City, the Hamptons and France.

The dedication ceremony was held November 17, 1997. The entrance tower stood nearly ninety feet high. When the terminal opened it was 344 feet in length which is slightly longer than a football field.

The wave ceiling on the second floor is 270 ft. x 50 ft., which is two and a half times the size of an Olympic swimming pool. The building had more than 30 ocean-inspired colors, including nine different shades of blue, and more than fifty Mickey Mouse images throughout the terminal building.

A host of Disney characters were depicted in the twenty-two bas relief panels atop the windows showing nautical adventures. Many of those details were removed during a renovation in 2011 to accommodate the Dream Class ships.

The building is set up unlike any other terminal since it is positioned at a perpendicular angle to the ship rather than the customary parallel one.

WDI development manager Kris Wilhelm said:

> If the ship is along the side of the building, as is typical, it blocks people's sightlines when they first see it. In orienting the building we realized we had a great photo opportunity if we turned the pier. It's unique not just to be unique. It ends up being a nice symmetry.

The 70,000 square foot terminal building was meant to balance form and function. In form, it captures an airy, friendly interior reminiscent of a classic passenger terminal with a 13,000 square foot terrazzo floor that is a map of the Caribbean Sea that originally included the DCL sailing routes, a twenty foot long 1/48th scale model of the *Disney Magic* cruise ship (with one side cut away to reveal the fully furnished interior) and other details capturing both a nautical feel as well as a Disney feel.

The ceiling has brushed aluminum panels simulating waves. A sixteen foot high Mickey Mouse head silhouette portal is near the station check-in counters as an entrance to board the ship.

In function, the terminal was designed to streamline both the embarkation and disembarking experience so that it was seamless.

To add to that seamless experience, Disney created the Disney Cruise Line buses to transport guests on the one hour ride from the airport or the WDW resorts. After researching Greyhound buses of the 1930s, Disney employed the HOK Studio E design firm who produced forty to fifty concept designs before settling on the final version.

Wilhelm said:

> The bus sets the tone. As soon as a guest gets on it, they know they are in a different time.

Ron Cohee started his Disney career as a Disney animator for Disney Feature Animation Florida before moving into Design Group (now known as Disney Creative Group). He worked on *Pocahontas, Mulan, Lilo and Stitch, The Princess and the Frog, John Henry, The Little Matchgirl,* and many others before Disney unwisely decided to eliminate the Florida studio and with it some talented artists.

Cohee is a passionate Disney fan, as well as an artist and has nothing but gratitude for his time at the Disney Company. He's worked on a ton of illustrated books for Pixar.

Regarding his career path, Cohee said:

> I attended the California Institute of the Arts from 1992-1994, and then worked at Disney Feature Animation for ten years, transferring to the Florida studio at one point along the way. After the studio closed in 2004, I worked at a smaller studio started by former Disney artists and added to my skills.
>
> I also kept busy freelancing for Disney Publishing and Walt Disney Imagineering; some of the buses at Walt Disney World are wrapped with my art, as is much of Disney's Art of Animation Resort, and ten of the wraps on the Skyliner gondolas. DDG graciously added me to their team in 2011 and I have been working for them ever since.

The art on the outside of the original DCL bus was redesigned by artist Ron Cohee, who told me:

I penciled the ducks—based partly on the dimensional figures on the stern of the *Disney Wonder* — and, when approved, inked and painted them digitally. I painted Mickey, as well, but it was a pre-existing pose.

On the stern of the Disney *Wonder*, Donald Duck is trying to paint the logo, while one of his nephews, Huey, is cutting away with a pair of scissors at one of the two ropes supporting the wooden swing Donald is on. Donald would then fall reasonably safely into the ocean with a comedic splash.

Cohee revealed:

> I couldn't do that same gag for the bus because then Donald would hit the pavement and that wouldn't be so funny. So I came up with a similar situation where Donald is helpless and one of the nephews is painting his tail while the other is preparing to throw a bucket of paint on him.

> And if you look closely, Donald is still in jeopardy of falling because one of the ropes has started to fray as in the original image, but not because of any maliciousness by the nephews.

In May 2019, Canaveral Port Authority and Disney Cruise Line reached a twenty year agreement to expand operations and make Port Canaveral home for two of Disney Cruise Line's three new ships and will be the home port for at least their first five years of operation.

This is a modification of an existing contract and comes with two additional five-year renewal options. Initially, Disney guarantees 150 sailings, but increases to 180 sailings in 2023 and up to 216 sailings in 2024 through the remainder of the 20-year term.

Jeff Vahle, president of Disney Cruise Line, said:

> Port Canaveral was the inaugural homeport for our first ship and has served as a gateway for magical cruise vacations ever since. We value our longstanding relationship with Port Canaveral and look forward to expanding our presence there as we introduce new ships and new family cruise experiences.

The terms of the new agreement continue Disney's exclusive operation from Cruise Terminal 8, in addition to providing preferential use of the Port's Cruise Terminal 10 for a third homeport vessel and during the months-long renovations of Terminal 8.

As part of the deal, Disney will begin paying the port what's known as a "capital cost recovery charge" of $3.15 per passenger getting on or off a Disney ship at Port Canaveral. This charge is designed to reimburse the port for the $46.5 million in terminal upgrades.

This fee will be in addition to a $7.98 per passenger wharfage charge Disney will pay the port, under terms of the new contract, plus dockage, line-handling and harbormaster fees.

For roughly several months starting in the summer of 2020, Cruise Terminal 8 will undergo a significant renovation at a cost of approximately forty-seven million dollars. The terminal will offer up to 1000 seats up from the current 384 and an expanded concierge waiting area.

The drop off area will also be expanded to better accommodate more cruise passengers arriving by car or using transportation services like vans. A new baggage screening area is planned to enable the security teams to process luggage more efficiently.

Disney Cruise Line will be moving towards a mobile check-in process of some sort which will allow the elimination of some of the check-in desks inside the terminal to be converted to guest seating. A new jet-way will be installed to accommodate the new class of ships that will dock at the port and a new Americans with Disabilities Act-compliant ramp will be installed for arriving passengers.

In the past, renovations to the terminal were done during the days the ship was at sea. BEA Architects Inc. of Miami will provide the land-side architectural and engineering design and permitting services at Terminals 8 and 10.

Disney Cruise Line has its own secured, well-lit parking lot and garage at Port Canaveral. The lot and garage have 24-hour security with cameras.

Walt Disney Theater

The Walt Disney Theatre spans three decks and can seat 977 guests onboard the *Disney Magic* and *Disney Wonder* and 1,340 guests on the *Disney Dream* and *Disney Fantasy*. The passenger capacity exceeds the seating for two shows a night but the expectation is that not every guest will go and see the show.

Vice President of Entertainment Jim Urry said:

> The theater is the heart of the ship and it rivals those in the West End or on Broadway. We've got a suspended balcony and by design,

we created a theater where viewing points are extremely clear. Very few seats have any kind of interference with the view of the stage. That was critical.

All the main stage theater shows are produced by Walt Disney Imagineering Creative Entertainment.

DCL was the first cruise line to utilize projection mapping in its theater starting in 2017. Eye Q Productions in California, had been creating projection mapping and animation for all sorts of projects since 2003. Their first project for Disney was in 2005 at Disneyland when it produced a show for the façade of the "it's a small world" attraction.

For the Walt Disney Theater shows, Eye Q produced images that extended beyond the sides of the stage and other things including for the pre-show of *The Golden Mickeys*, the animation of Disney characters filling empty seats in the theater shown on the screen.

They had to create special mounts to hold the ten projectors in place for alignment to compensate for any rocking of the ship. In addition, they had to compensate for the color palette of the red and gold surfaces on the walls of the theater so that the images do not have the same colors that would blend in to those particular colors.

Among the leading-edge technical effects in the Walt Disney Theatre is an infrared camera with motion tracking, allowing the movement of performers to be blended with projected digital animated effects.

Some of the previous Walt Disney Theater stage shows included:
- *Disney Wishes* (A musical journey about three best friends who discover with segments from classic animated Disney features that the secret to being a grown-up is staying connected to their inner child by being young at heart.)
- *Hercules: The Muse-ical* (The Muses retell the story of the 1997 animated feature with some "vaudevillian" self-referential humor.)
- *Villains Tonight* (The Fates tell Hades that he will lose his position as Lord of the Underworld unless he ramps up his evil so he turns to some classic Disney villains and sinister sidekicks for help.)
- *Toy Story—The Musical* (Six new songs in this tale of Andy 6th birthday present of Buzz Lightyear trying to fit in with Woody and the other toys.)

The Deck 3 lobby entrance to the Walt Disney Theater on the *Disney Dream* has a huge photo of Walt Disney and is also used for passengers to interact with costumed characters, or be tempted by the nearby merchandise shops.

Most guests are unaware of The Disney Zodiac overhead. It is a very detailed circular piece of brass artwork where Disney characters represent the signs of the zodiac.

Obviously, it was difficult to find perfect matches for each sign but whoever came up with the final choices did fairly well and certainly made me smile.

Here is the identification chart I put together:

- Aries (The Ram): Merlin as a goat (*Sword in the Stone*)
- Taurus (The Bull): Ferdinand (from 1938 short *Ferdinand the Bull*)
- Gemini (The Twins): Si and Am (Siamese cats from *Lady and the Tramp*)
- Cancer (The Crab): Sebastian (*The Little Mermaid*)
- Leo (The Lion): Adult Simba (*The Lion King*)
- Virgo (The Maiden/Virgin): Princess Aurora (*Sleeping Beauty*)
- Libra (The Scales): Rafiki (*The Lion King*)
- Scorpio (The Scorpion): Hades (*Hercules*)
- Sagittarius (The Archer): Robin Hood (*Robin Hood*, 1973)
- Capricorn (The Goat): Djali (*The Hunchback of Notre Dame*)
- Aquarius (The Water Bearer): Ariel (*The Little Mermaid*)
- Pisces (The Fish): Flounder (*The Little Mermaid*)

Pirate Night and Fireworks

Captain Mary Oceaneer, a member of the Society of Explorers and Adventures (S.E.A.) is the founder of the Oceaneer Labs aboard the *Disney Magic* and *Disney Wonder*. She is a treasure hunter and diver accompanied by her pet parrot Salty. The maiden voyage of her Oceaneer Lab ship took place on July 30th, 1898 (a reference to the *Disney Magic's* maiden voyage in 1998) and uncovered buried treasure on Castaway Cay.

Her appearance on the ships inspired the creation of the Miss Adventure Falls raft ride attraction at WDW's Typhoon Lagoon.

With treasure hunting being her main occupation, she developed a fondness for pirate lore and would establish special "Pirate Nights" aboard her vessel to allow her crew to have fun and blow off some steam.

A painting of the first "Pirate Night" in 1898 holds a prominent spot in the "Craft Studio" and shipping crates are labeled as containing remains of Shipwreck Cove and the Dead Man's Chest can also be found in the area.

It is doubtful that many if any adult passengers know this back story, especially if they travel without children or on the *Dream* or *Fantasy*.

In actuality, it is not difficult to make the connection between the DCL voyages being made into the Caribbean and the iconic Disney theme park attraction Pirates of the Caribbean and its later film franchise. Pirate Night occurs on all Bahamas and Caribbean DCL voyages.

Walt Disney told author Bob Thomas that when he was a student in Marceline, Missouri, he remembered reading Robert Louis Stevenson's *Treasure Island* novel in class and was so enthralled with the tale that his imaginary encounters with pirate Long John Silver not only filled his thoughts in English class but the daydreams carried over to his algebra class the next period.

His older brother Roy recalled Walt spending time playing at being a pirate on a small island in the nearby Yellow Creek River. Walt went on to produce several films that prominently featured pirates including *Treasure Island* (1950), *Swiss Family Robinson* (1960), *Blackbeard's Ghost* (1968) and, of course, the animated feature *Peter Pan* (1953) that enhanced the mythology of Captain Hook and his pirate crew.

Walt was personally responsible for the creation of the iconic Pirates of the Caribbean attraction at Disneyland, even supplying the name for it. That attraction inspired the film *Pirates of the Caribbean: Curse of the Black Pearl* (2003) that introduced the pirate scoundrel Captain Jack Sparrow and spawned a multi-film franchise. Sparrow and some other elements from the film were later incorporated into the attraction.

On the *Disney Magic* and *Disney Wonder*, the emphasis is more on the classic Fab Five characters in pirate attire where Pirate Mickey is more of an adventurer than a scoundrel and knave.

The *Disney Dream* and *Disney Fantasy* focus more on Captain Jack Sparrow but without any other characters from the film franchise.

Pirate Night on the ship starts in the afternoon with various activities including Pirates Flash Mob Rehearsal, Disney Junior Pirate & Princess Dance Party, Pirate Trivia and crafts, Meet & Greet with Pirate characters, Pirate Games among other additions including pirate-themed background music throughout the ship.

On Pirate Night the Main Dining Rooms feature a pirate or Caribbean themed menu not available any other day including jerk chicken and rum cake. Servers are dressed in pirate attire.

After the fireworks, there is a special half hour Pirates Buffet in Cabanas that is not well known. It includes items like turkey legs, tacos, loaded potato bar, crepes and other treats. The location features pirate themed food displays like carved watermelons and cantaloupes that look like pirate faces.

There is a deck party with a short stage show in the pool area below the funnel vision screen before the fireworks. After the fireworks, the same area hosts the family friendly Club Pirate Dance Party.

For many guests, Pirate Night is a major reason for booking a Disney cruise. Often, they bring elaborate pirate costumes (some easily and inexpensively available on Amazon.com) while others opt for a simple pirate-themed t-shirt. The ships do not sell pirate costumes for adults. Some people recommend buying pirate outfits at a discount the day after Halloween and then storing them for the cruise.

However, there are pirate costumes for children available for sale. In addition, Bibbidi Bobbidi Boutique is transformed for one day only into The Pirates League. Children and adults can have make-up done and receive a few accessories like an eye patch. For a higher price, children can get a full costume.

On the day of Pirate Night, the stateroom attendant will leave edible chocolate coins covered in a gold wrapping rather than the usual Ghiradelli milk chocolate square. Additional coins are available for free that evening at the Guest Services desk.

In addition, a red Pirate Mickey bandana is also placed on the guest's bed. Over the years, the bandana has gotten smaller so it may not comfortably fit all heads which is why some guests bring their own (also available at Amazon.com).

It is simple to tie a bandana like a pirate. Fold the bandana into a triangle by bringing the two opposite corners together. Lay the bandana flat on solid surface like a tabletop. Smooth out any bunches or wrinkles.

Smooth hair back so that it doesn't stick out of the front of the bandana or bunches up inside it. Pick up the folded bandana with the point of the triangle pointing upward. Place the flat edge of the bandana on the forehead, on or near the hairline.

Take the two opposite tapering ends and tie a knot at the back of the head. Keep the edge of the bandana above the ears. Tie the ends together in a square knot. Make sure the bandana isn't too tight or too loose.

Tuck in the corner point of the bandana under the knot where you tied it. Smooth out any stray hair that might be sticking out.

Buccaneer Blast takes place about 10:30pm and Disney describes it as "a spectacular display of piratical pyrotechnics."

Disney Cruise Line was the first and only cruise line to offer fireworks on cruises fleet-wide. Disney had to go through lots of red tape to get permission and make concessions to do fireworks at sea. For instance, the fireworks shell casings are all made out of biodegradable materials that fish could eat, so that whatever pieces might fall into the water wouldn't cause any problems to the ocean life.

The fireworks are launched from the ship itself in a safe area on top of the second funnel by a patented air compressor rather than a fuse which reduces the risk of fire or accident. The display appears over the starboard (right) side of the ship.

DCL must launch all fireworks before entering back into the United States. Therefore if they can not launch them for Pirate night due to the weather or other conditions they must be disposed of properly before entering back into the United States.

They must alert all surrounding ships that they are going to be launching fireworks and when they will be starting, how many and any changes. Starting about 5-10 minutes before they must give the coast guard 30 second updates on what is happening so it will not be confused with distress signal flares.

The ships have a system which shuts the fireworks off as soon as something goes wrong. The fireworks are stored with the pyro for the stage shows and there is a limit to the total quantity of pyro that can be stored. So if a show needs more pyro, that limits the amount available for the fireworks display and vice versa.

In May 2013 Norwegian Cruise Line started an environmentally-friendly pyrotechnics display on every cruise of its ship Norwegian Breakaway (and later Norwegian Getaway) as the finale of a 1980s-themed deck party. They ended the fireworks display in August 2015 because of expense and labor once again making Disney the only cruise line offering a fireworks show.

It is well known that other cruise lines have been known to position their ships near a DCL cruise ship on the nights featuring fireworks for their passengers to see the display although not hear the Disney background music. There are no fireworks on the Alaska cruises because of environmental restrictions including the potential harm to wildlife and proximity to the land.

AquaDuck

The AquaDuck is a water coaster rather than a water slide that can be found on both the *Disney Dream* and the *Disney Fantasy*. It was the cruise line industry's first water coaster.

It's a 765-feet long translucent acrylic tube, and there is a loop that actually goes out 12 feet or so beyond the side of the ship at a height of about 150 feet over the surface of the ocean where guests can look straight down to the ocean's surface.

The water flows at a rate of 10,000 gallons per minute, so the trip is only about a minute, but the person in a rubber raft is propelled at about twenty feet a second and through the front funnel. Water jets are used for upward propulsion.

According to the Imagineering back story, Donald Duck's nephews (Huey, Dewey and Louie) built the ride, but Donald insisted on trying it before it was completely finished and he ended up stuffed in one of the ship's funnels with only his three-dimensional rear end visible to guests just as in the finale of WDW's attraction Mickey's PhilharMagic. In actuality, AquaDuck was inspired by the Walt Disney World Resort's Typhoon Lagoon.

Show Producer and Production Manager Peter Ricci said:

> AquaDuck combines a water blaster with the Lazy River, and we elevated it, so it wouldn't take up much deck space. You whisk through a 270-degree loop that extends twelve feet over the side of the ship.
>
> You then accelerate back uphill, through a clear acrylic tube about fifty-four inches in diameter. It's not confining at all and that it's clear makes it all the more inviting. You zoom along at

about fourteen feet per second, but that will vary depending on where you are in the ride. Then you descend and whip through the forward funnel, where there's a lighting effect.

You are inside the 'tween club Edge and the kids inside can see the silhouettes of riders hurtling by. Then you go into a not-so-lazy river that is about 7,000 to 9,000 gallons of water coming down through a pipe. This takes you whizzing down around the other funnel and into our splashdown lane.

The original idea of just a Lazy River, like at WDW's Typhoon Lagoon water park, came from Imagineers Joe Lanzisero and Bruce Vaughn but was rejected because water is heavy and it would have put too much weight on the very top of the ship. AquaDuck is a reference to the ancient Roman aqueducts that populated the European landscape and were used to transport water.

For the maiden voyage of the *Disney Dream* in 2011, a costumed character Donald Duck christened the AquaDuck during a special ceremony where water was added to the AquaDuck from both Typhoon Lagoon and Blizzard Beach.

Disney Creative Group artist Ron Cohee at Walt Disney World did the series of murals in the queue on the way up to the AquaDuck. He was instructed that Donald Duck needed to wear swim trunks, which presented a challenge. The end gag is Donald getting stuck in the ship's forward funnel on Deck 12 with his naked rear end and orange webbed feet clearly visible.

So Cohee had to figure out a way for Donald to logically lose his trunks in the last panel. Basically, the nephews increase the force of the water pushing him out of the tube and it apparently pulls off his swim trunks.

The mural states:

> AquaDuck: Duck In - Fly Out: Donald's nephews built this slide... and uncle wanted the first ride. They were worried he'd get stuck... but he sailed like an Aquaduck.

For children not tall enough to ride the AquaDuck, there is a Mickey Slide in the children's pool and in Nemo's Reef, a water play area and for even smaller children including those still in diapers, there is a small slide inspired by Mr. Ray from Pixar's *Finding Nemo*. The blue body of the stingray was perfectly proportioned for a mini-slide.

When DCL decided to add an upper deck water feature to the *Disney Magic*, they created more of a true water slide without a raft called the AquaDunk. The floor beneath the guest who crosses their hands across their chest opens up beneath them and they plummet straight down and curve around twenty feet over the side of the ship for seven seconds before splashing down.

Environmental Overview

Each Disney ship has an onboard Environmental Officer dedicated to overseeing all environmental systems and procedures, along with water reclamation efforts. These officers monitor the ship's overall water quality and supply, train all officers and crew members on waste minimization and environmental safety programs and oversee multiple environmental initiatives, including all shipboard recycling efforts.

Shipboard recycling processes have helped to eliminate more than 2,100 tons of metals, glass, plastic and paper from traditional waste streams since 2014. Each stateroom on all four Disney Cruise Line ships contains a recycling bin for plastic, paper and aluminum.

Condensation from the shipboard air conditioning units is collected and re-used to wash the decks and for the laundry facilities, saving more than 30 million gallons of water each year.

Excess heat from power generators is used to run evaporators, which, combined with other shipboard initiatives, transform approximately 142,000 gallons of seawater into potable water on board each of the ships every day.

All DCL ships feature Advanced Wastewater Purification Systems (AWPS) that utilize natural processes to treat and purify onboard wastewater to levels far exceeding international shipping standards.

Disney Cruise Line made history by being the first cruise line to utilize an innovative hull coating that is both 100 percent nontoxic to the marine environment, and effective in increasing fuel efficiency. The coating helps reduce the ships' surface resistance in the water, decreasing the need for propulsion power as the ship glides through the sea.

Crew members use biodegradable cleaning products wherever possible, avoiding potentially harmful phosphates and other chemicals associated with traditional cleaners.

More than 1,000 gallons of used cooking oil from shipboard galleys is offloaded and recycled in ports of call around the world each week. Through a unique partnership with Bahamas Waste Management (BWM) in Nassau, the used cooking oil is being converted into biodiesel fuel used to power a local fleet of BWM vehicles.

Shipboard recycling systems help divert more than 325 tons of aluminum, plastics, paper and non-traditional recyclables from conventional waste streams each year. That's the equivalent of over 54 school buses or 24 humpback whales.

Disney Cruise Line has eliminated plastic straws, cutlery, stirrers, shopping bags and condiment packets. Disposable polystyrene cups have also been replaced with insulated paper cups. And in an effort to reduce the use of plastic bottles, refillable waters stations have been installed fleet wide in both guest and Crew Member areas. Additionally, all guest staterooms now feature large, refillable bath product dispensers.

Disney Cruise Line and Disney Animal Programs have partnered with local non-profit organizations, Disney researchers and educators in a multi-year project to restore the health of the coral reefs around Castaway Cay, Disney's private island, and throughout The Bahamas. Researchers are taking long-spined sea urchins that are native to the area and trans-locating them to coral reefs endangered by algae overgrowth. The sea urchins graze on algae similar to a lawnmower keeping the grass short.

Crew members partner with experts from Disney's Animals, Science and Environment Team to protect and monitor loggerhead sea turtle nests on Castaway Cay. Their efforts have helped protect this endangered species.

Disney Cruise Line voluntarily participates in a program to record sightings of humpback whales off the coast of Alaska for the National Oceanic and Atmospheric Administration (NOAA) during summer sailings. DCL is dedicated to avoiding interactions with marine life. DCL complies with voluntary seasonal shipping lane changes, voluntary reporting and ship speed reductions. Prior to each season in Alaska, DCL also conduct marine life avoidance refresher training for the captains and first officers to help them with recognizing whale types, their behavior, and migratory patterns, which is the first step in avoiding interactions.

As of 2019, the environmental programs of Disney Cruise Line have eliminated more than 6,400 tons of metals, glass, plastic and paper from traditional waste streams through recycling, removed more than 31,000 pounds of trash and debris from beaches and waterways and inspired more than 7,200 children in The Bahamas and the Cayman Islands through participation in environmental educational programs.

Disney Channel Mickey Mouse Cartoons

One channel on the stateroom television sets is devoted to a loop of Mickey Mouse cartoons produced by Disney Television Animation for the Disney Channel. One of the cartoons on the loop is the 2017 episode entitled *Shipped Out* that makes fun of the V.I.P. cruise experience.

This new series was announced in March 2013 with the first short (*No Service*) premiering on The Disney Channel on June 28. Actor Chris Diamantopoulos rather than Bret Iwan voices Mickey Mouse. Other voice performers include Russi Taylor, Tony Anselmo, Bill Farmer, Jim Cummings, Corey Burton, April Winchell and Tress MacNeille.

The series is created by a thirty-person team in Burbank and an animation team in Canada using Flash software called Harmony, with background done in Photoshop.

Currently there are over a hundred color cartoons, each running three-and-a-half minutes (rather than the usual seven minutes for the classic Mickey Mouse cartoons), with one of them seven minutes long and two half hour specials. Each cartoon finds Mickey in a different contemporary setting such as Santa Monica, New York, Paris, Beijing, Tokyo, Venice, and the Alps, facing a silly situation, a quick complication, and an escalation of physical and visual gags.

The concept was to capture the spirit and the wild slapstick fun of the early black-and-white Mickey Mouse cartoon shorts.

Emmy Award-winning artist and director Paul Rudish (*Star Wars: Clone Wars*, *Dexter's Laboratory*, *Powerpuff Girls*) is the creator, executive producer and occasional director of the series. His father Rich created the character of Rainbow Brite for Hallmark.

Senior vice president Eric Coleman told animation historian and author Jerry Beck:

The goal is to introduce Mickey to a new generation of kids and at the same time entertain their parents who have their memories of Mickey Mouse. Our intention is to highlight his personality and show him as the star he has always been.

Making them feel contemporary doesn't mean give them an iPhone and headphones; it's the execution, the sensibility, the tone, the way they are animated, the music the movement, the timing, the editing. We wanted to make shorts that would play well globally. We have Disney Channels around the world.

The series has won multiple Emmy and Annie awards and inspired the new attraction at Disneyland and Walt Disney World, Mickey and Minnie's Runaway Railway.

At the beginning of the ride, guests will be invited to watch the premiere of a new Mickey Mouse cartoon entitled *Perfect Picnic* made by the same team that makes the Disney Channel shorts.

Mickey, Minnie and Pluto prepare for a picnic outing and encounter Goofy as the engineer on a train. A hole appears in the movie screen and guests board the train cars for a trackless ride experience inside the wacky and unpredictable cartoon that includes projection mapping and physical audio-animatronics figures.

Christopher Willis, who is the composer for the Mickey shorts, has created background loops for the queue made up of his favorite themes from the cartoons, but with a classic Hollywood feel. He also composed a brand new theme song for the attraction.

Captain Minnie

Disney ships are the only cruise ships to have five official captains: the ship's captain, Captain Mickey, Captain Hook and Captain Jack Sparrow. Captain Minnie Mouse was introduced in April 2019 meant to empower young girls and "inspire the next generation of female leaders in the maritime industry."

Minnie's uniform of white trousers or a white skirt paired with a red jacket marks her first time ever wearing pants on a regular basis as an official costume.

In 2019, DCL sponsored four scholarships at the LJM Maritime Academy in The Bahamas for female cadets who aspire to be ship captains and shipboard leaders. The scholarships, one for each of the ships in the Disney Cruise Line fleet, include tuition to the three-year program. The scholarships included two years of study at the academy and one year of service aboard a Disney ship.

Jeff Vahle, president of Disney Cruise Line, said:

> Our Disney characters have a unique ability to inspire and connect with children, and we know Captain Minnie will encourage young girls around the world to consider a career in the maritime industry. We are excited to work with LJM Maritime Academy to offer scholarships for young women who are pursuing their passions and following their dreams in our industry.

As part of a commitment to encourage future generations to pursue careers in the maritime industry, Captain Minnie Mouse visits children in some of Disney Cruise Line's homeports and ports of call.

As part of these local community visits, Captain Minnie Mouse is accompanied by a female Disney Cruise Line officer or crew member to showcase their roles in the maritime industry and raise awareness about career choices for women aboard a cruise ship.

DCL unveiled a special line of merchandise, exclusive to the Disney fleet spotlighting Captain Minnie. Items in the nautical-themed collection of apparel and gifts feature the tagline, "You Can Call Me Captain." A brand-new Captain Minnie Mouse plush was recently introduced.

In the future, young girls will get to dress the part with a Captain Minnie Mouse makeover at Bibbidi Bobbidi Boutique, available exclusively on Disney ships. According to Disney publicity, "At this special salon, children can transform into seafaring captains, inspired by their favorite mouse."

Disney Wish

At a 2016 Walt Disney Company Annual Meeting of Shareholders, Bob Iger announced there would be a new ship added to the DCL fleet. During a June 2018 Port Canaveral meeting, it was mentioned that the new ship would homeport there making cruises beginning in January 2022 although it will be delivered in late 2021.

During the 2019 D23 Expo, Disney Parks, Experiences and Products Chairman Bob Chapek announced the ship would be named the *Disney Wish* and showed concept art of the three-story atrium supposedly inspired by enchanted fairy tales:

There couldn't be a better name for our incredible new ship because making wishes come true is part of the Disney DNA and is at the heart of so many of our cherished stories. The ship's stern will feature Rapunzel. Spirited, smart, curious and above all, adventurous, Rapunzel embodies the wish and desire to see and experience the world.

Accompanying Rapunzel from the Disney animated feature *Tangled* will be her talented sidekick, the chameleon Pascal. Rapunzel's enchanted hair will suspend the character as she decorates the stern. A Rapunzel stage show and restaurant are featured on the *Disney Magic*.

The *Disney Wish* hull number is s.705 and is being built at Meyer Werft in Germany that had built the *Disney Dream* and *Disney Fantasy*. The ship will be powered by clean-burning liquefied natural gas. By moving to natural gas propulsion instead of oil-based fuel, cruise ships are able to reduce emissions of sulfur, nitrogen oxide and other chemicals.

The ship will be approximately 140,000 gross tons, with 1,250 guest staterooms planned for a maximum 4000 passengers. It will be 1,119 feet long making it slightly larger than the *Disney Dream* and *Disney Fantasy*. The speculation is that the added space might be used to increase the size of the staterooms or provide more public space with additional activities.

The ship will also have a connection with the Make A Wish Foundation. The Walt Disney Company has a forty year history with the foundation, granting 130,000 "wishes" for children with terminal illnesses since 1980. Disney is not only the largest wish-granter in existence, but was part of the very first wish granted by Make-A-Wish Foundation and continues to grant 9,000 in tandem with the non-profit each and every year.

The *Disney Wish* will be one of three new ships that will be designated Triton Class. The two other ships (hull numbers s.718 and s.706), unnamed at this time, will be delivered in 2022 and 2023.

Chapek added:

> Each Disney Cruise Line ship is unique, with a name that embodies the excitement of sailing with Disney and the power of our stories. The new ships will have the experiences our guests love, as well as all-new magic.

SEAcrets of the Ships

Pepe's Cabin. The Muppet character Pepe the King Prawn, who has a major role in one of the DCL ship's Midship Detective Agency interactive adventures, has his very own stateroom on the *Disney Fantasy* and *Disney Dream*.

Located at the end of the hall on Deck 5 Aft from the Oceaneer Club and Lab, the half-sized door to stateroom 5148 ½ is decorated with his activity schedule, photos of his Muppet friends and notes from guests. The door remains locked and closed since Pepe is out participating in the detective activity.

The door includes his photo with a note to call him at "41-5148", a list of excursions with color photos of various Muppets participating, and a betting form for Pepe's Crab Races with the crab names and the Muppets who bet on each one: Sandy Claws (Rizzo), Chum Runner (Pepe), Old Bay (Bobo), Sebastian (Pepe), and Peewee Hermit (Lew Zealand).

In addition, there is a list posted of the Muppet Mini Golf Team ("You're tee-riffic!"): Fozzie, Statler & Waldorf, Gonzo, Beauregard and Bingo winners.

According to his ABC television official biography, Pepino Rodrigo Serrano Gonzales was born off the coast of Mallorca, Spain and became a chef before immigrating to the United States to try to find a career in show business in Hollywood.

The four-armed Pepe takes offense if mistaken for a shrimp. He speaks with a heavy Spanish accent, often ending his sentences with the word "...okay?" Puppeteer Bill Barretta, who created the character in 1996, based the accent on his wife's aunt. One of the reasons for his prominence on the ship is his relationship to the sea.

Pepe frequently hosts DVD extra material and being the spokesprawn for the fast food restaurant chain Long John Silver's commercials besides appearing in film and video projects. He is known as an inveterate schemer and ladies' man.

Buttons. Several DCL specific buttons are available at the Guest Services desk for free by request. They are roughly about 2/3rd the size of the buttons available at Walt Disney World Guest Relations desks or basically two and a half inches in circumference.

The buttons include "I'm Celebrating" (with colorful Mickey head balloons floating), "Just Graduated" (with a motor board flung high in the sky with confetti), "Happy Birthday" (with an iced birthday cake and four lit candles. On one cruise with students I got the buttons for all of them and using the black marker available at the desk changed them into "UnBirthday" buttons in reference to the party in *Alice in Wonderland*), "Happy Anniversary" (with Mickey and Minnie holding hands) and "Happily Ever After" (with two exploding fireworks creating entwined hearts in the night sky).

The most popular button is "Magical Moments" (with the image of a gold porthole and inside it the picture of a DCL ship with Tinker Bell overhead pixie dusting it). A previous "Magical Moments" blue button had Tinker Bell in the center and the phrase "Where dreams come true." At the bottom of each button it says "Disney Cruise Line". There is no "First Voyage" button.

If a child loses a tooth, there is a "I Lost a Tooth" button (with the grinning face of the Cheshire Cat who has a missing tooth). Guest Relations will also supply a certificate and sometimes a gift like a pin or a plush if notified of a lost tooth. Tinker Bell takes care of all lost teeth on the ship.

Cast members have conflicting stories about why she does it including that the Tooth Fairy can't fly out to sea to retrieve the tooth so since Tink is always on the ship has designated her as the surrogate. Another version is that Tink is so possessive that she won't allow another fairy into her territory at sea.

Over the years, there have been DCL buttons celebrating Castaway Cay Crab Races (with the image of Sebastian), Maiden Voyage (with Mickey as Steamboat Willie in full color), a Disney Dream button with Sorcerer Mickey celebrating the ship's Spring 2011 debut, a Disney Fantasy button with Dumbo flying over the ship wearing a captain's hat and holding a DCL pennant with his trunk celebrating the debut of the ship in 2012,

Sailor Goofy (from the cartoon *How to Be a Sailor* tipping his cap for a "I'm Celebrating" button), Happy 5th birthday (in celebration of the *Disney Magic*, Castaway Cay and *Disney Wonder* with Captain Mickey in his red captain uniform saluting), DVC buttons like a gold porthole with an image of the ship and the phrase "Our members are going places" and one with Pluto in a sailor cap and the phrase "I know the 'Sea'cret".

For Disney movie premieres at sea like *Meet the Robinsons, Brother Bear, Bolt,* and *Cars* ("The Ultimate Off Road Trip") among other special events buttons were issued.

Pressed Pennies. The only pressed penny machine is in the boarding cruise terminal at Port Canaveral between the check-in desks and boarding gate. You won't be able to access it when you get off the ship, so if you want them, you have to get them before you board.

The pressed coin machine was installed at Disney Cruise Line's terminal at Port Canaveral in the fall of 2013. There are a total of six designs to collect, including one for each ship and one featuring Castaway Cay featuring Mickey and Minnie in beach chairs on the island with the ship docked in the background. The last design features a full figured Captain Mickey standing next to a DCL cruise ship.

Magic features a full figured Sorcerer Mickey. *Wonder* features full figured Steamboat Willie Mickey. *Dream* features waist high Captain Mickey saluting. *Fantasy* features waist high Sorcerer Mickey with arms outstretched.

Each pressed penny costs fifty-one cents. The machine includes a built-in change machine to get quarters, but you will need to bring your own pennies and to be safe your own quarters.

Newer, uncirculated pennies that have the shield on the back instead of the monument building and minted after 1982 usually produce a brighter, better looking image although some zinc may show through in the final pressing.

Disney Crew Members. The crew members are on contracts lasting four to nine months. At the end of the contract, they can choose to extend for another six months with no time off or with a set amount of time for a break usually six weeks. Crew members receive month long extensive training in Canada for medical emergencies, life boat drills, fire safety and more. Crew members are frequently retested on safety procedures at any time and can be terminated for not passing.

Crew members also receive job-specific training and usually share a tiny cabin below decks with several other members from their same department. The crew is primarily international with just a miniscule percentage of Americans.

There is an exclusive crew pool at the front of the ship that also serves as a party and socializing area for crew. In addition, there is a crew gym, bar lounge and mess that also serves as a location for meetings and gatherings. Meetings can be scheduled at 2am in the morning because that is when most of the crew rarely interacts with the guests.

Crew members get food and lodging, travel and the opportunity to make friends with about sixty or so different nationalities working on board. On the other hand, salary is considered fairly low although overtime pay is available. Crew members can work seventy hours a week under challenging conditions.

Application and the interview process are different for all candidates as it can depend on the country they live in and the position they are applying for on the ship. Information on jobs as well as some explanatory videos are available at the website: https://jobs.disneycareers.com/disney-cruise-line.

Tall Tale. At 1,115 feet each, the *Disney Fantasy* and *Disney Dream* are longer than the height of the Eiffel Tower in Paris (1,063 feet) and longer than the height of New York City's famous Chrysler Building (1,047 feet). The *Disney Magic* and *Disney Wonder* are each longer than Main Street U.S.A at the Magic Kingdom in Walt Disney World.

See the Light. A "light point" is a term that shipbuilders use for "anything that's a light." There are approximately 80,000 light points on the *Disney Fantasy* and *Disney Dream*— "double the normal number for a ship this size," according to Meyer Werft, the shipyard in Germany where the *Disney Fantasy* and *Disney Dream* were built using primarily LEDs and other environmentally friendly lighting.

The Ship's Horn. The horn on each ship is able to play the first two lines from the song "When You Wish Upon a Star" from *Pinocchio* (1940). With the launch of the *Disney Dream* in 2011, the Disney ships added to their repertoire the first line from "Yo Ho! Yo Ho! (A Pirate's Life for Me)" from the Pirates of the Caribbean theme park attraction, "It's a Small World "from the Disney park attraction, "Be Our Guest" from *Beauty and the Beast* (1991), "Hi Diddle Dee Dee (An Actor's Life for Me)" from *Pinocchio* (1940) and "A Dream is a Wish Your Heart Makes" from *Cinderella* (1950). In October 2015, the song "Do You Want to Build a Snowman?" from *Frozen* (2013) was added to the horn's musical repertoire.

The *Disney Magic* and *Disney Wonder* use the "old" air horns. They each have seven of them. The *Disney Fantasy* and *Disney Dream* broadcast a digital reproduction of the sound through loud speakers.

Funnel Vision. Funnel Vision is a large LED screen mounted outside on the rear funnel near the main pool. On it, movies, sporting events and material as a backdrop for the deck shows are screened. On the *Magic* and the *Wonder* it is approximately 24 by 14 feet. On the *Dream* and *Fantasy*, it is approximately 30 feet by 18 feet. In the evening, the pool is covered and some guests sit in deck chairs to watch what is being shown. At first, DCL intended to call it Ariel View, referencing The Little Mermaid.

KTTW. The Key to the World Card has a RFID (Radio Frequency IDentifier) chip embedded in it to unlock the stateroom door and was meant to be placed in a metal slot just inside the doorway to turn on the lights and air conditioning. Veteran cruisers have learned to bring an old gift card (with no remaining credit) or hotel card to put in the slot and sometimes put a small piece of magnetic tape on the back at the top of the card so it will stick to the wall when not in use. The KTTC also lists dining rotation order, lifeboat station and is used by the ship's photographers to group your onboard photos together into an account.

Disney at Sea with D23. This thirty minute entertainment news show in the Buena Vista Theater highlights what is new and what is coming to all things Disney from theme parks to movies, television, music and more. The show is updated every month.

D23's Michael Vargo said:

> Our friends at Disney Cruise Line reached out and asked us to develop a show that would take guests on a journey through all the incredible entertainment and experiences coming from Disney, Pixar, Marvel, and Lucasfilm. It's thrilling to share all of the exciting news—and our love for Disney—with our guests on the high seas.

Goofy Golf: Disney Design Group artist Ron Cohee did the artwork for the Goofy mini-golf area on the Sports Deck (Deck 13 aft) of the *Disney Dream*. In the area is a basketball court, ping pong tables, digital sports simulators and the nine-hole miniature golf course that include comical "lessons" by Goofy and his son, Max. For instance, Pluto's dog bone will guide you to the hole, but try to avoid the fire hydrants in Handling a Dog Leg. You grab a club from "Max's Country Clubs" bag and the golf balls are, of course, labeled as "GoofBalls".

The area was inspired by the Goofy short cartoon *How to Golf* (1944) which was another installment in the popular a series cartoons where a narrator explains the fundamentals of a sport while visually Goofy completely messes up. Another inspiration was the episode *Tee for Two* (November 1992) from the animated series *Goof Troop* where Pete tries to tear down a miniature golf course and Goofy and Max stop him.

Disney Magic Chandelier. The grand atrium lobby features colors of the sea, like coral, blue and aquamarine. The carpet is a seashell design. In January 2014 while in drydock the original Chihuly chandelier was replaced with an easier to maintain and clean integrated-into-the-ceiling chandelier that represents the golden yellow rays of the sun shining above an undersea garden. The Helmsman Mickey statue was also repositioned when it was in drydock when one of the atrium staircases was removed.

Disney Fantasy Chandelier. The chandelier cascades downward from a massive, illuminated stained-glass flourish on the ceiling in vibrant hues of greens and blues. The chandelier itself is more than ten feet in diameter, a one-of-a-kind work of art evoking a peacock in stained glass and more than 60,000 clear Swarovski crystal beads.

Disney Dream Chandelier. The chandelier sparkles with thousands of hand-crafted crystal beads and glows with colorful glasswork. Crafted in Brixen, located in Northern Italy, the chandelier is 22 feet in diameter at the ceiling plate and comes down 13 feet from the ceiling. It is 24kt gold plated with a total of 88,680 Swarovski crystal beads ranging in size from 6mm to 12mm.

Rival Ship Godmothers. Disney Legend Julie Andrews is the godmother of a rival cruise ship, *Crystal Serenity*, and Disney Legend Angela Lansbury is the godmother of the *Crystal Symphony*. Both ships are part of the American Crystal Cruises founded in 1988.

Cruise Cartoon. *Shipped Out* is the sixty-fourth episode and the sixth episode in season 4 of the Disney Channel Mickey Mouse cartoons. It debuted August 25, 2017 and is included in the Mickey Mouse cartoons shown on the stateroom television. Written by Darrick Bachman, Paul Rudish, Dave Wasson and directed by Wasson.

It tells the story of an exhausted Mickey Mouse and Minnie taking a cruise vacation to relax. They have booked the all-inclusive V.I.P. experience so red-headed, perky cruise director Erica (voice of Illya Owens) and her subordinates force them into a variety of high energy "fun" activities including bungie jumping, gourmet food sampling, rock climbing, paint ball, participating in a stage show and more.

While the ship has the colors of the DCL ship, the experience is meant to parody the offerings on the Royal Caribbean due to the inclusion of the FlowRider, the bowl slide, the SkyFly and more that exist on that cruise line but not on the DCL. In the end a disasterous fireworks demonstration while parasailing leaves Mickey and Minnie happily secluded on a deserted island where they can relax as the ship sails away.

Safety First. Safety is a priority on DCL with the crew receiving extensive and continuing training. *Safety Smart: On the Go!* Is a series of animated shorts based on the *Wild About Safety* episodes featuring the characters of Timon & Pumbaa offering safety tips.

In a two minute *Safety Smart: On the Go*! short devoted to boat safety, a DCL cruise ship is shown frequently in the background and references are made to safety measures on a cruise ship including the importance of life jackets.

This short series is displayed on television monitors in the lobby of the resorts in Walt Disney World and Disneyland. These educational short films were produced by Disney Educational Productions, Duck Soup Studios and Underwriters Laboratories. The series is directed and produced by Dave Bossert, and written by Douglas Segal.

Checking In With Goofy. In February 2011, DCL released a two minute promotional webtoon done in Flash animation entitled *Checkin' In With Goofy*. It is done in the style of the classic "How To..." animated shorts featuring Goofy to show people how easy it is to check in to embark on a Disney Cruise. The narrator is Corey Burton imitating John McLeish the original narrator for the 1940s shorts. (It is posted on YouTube as "Goofy Presents How to Take a Disney Cruise".)

The premise of the cartoon is that Goofy has a nightmare that there is so much paperwork to fill out at the terminal that he literally misses his ship. In reality, the cartoon points out the required paperwork can easily be done at home on the internet including picking a boarding time.

When Goofy is filling in his cruise paperwork he is standing between the characters Roger and Anita from *101 Dalmatians*. There is a Hidden Mickey head on Goofy's computer. According to his check-in information, Goofy lives at the same address where the Walt Disney Animation Studio in Burbank is located. As the ship pulls away, the audience can see that it is the *Disney Dream*.

Besides the DCL ships including things like a Goofy Pool, Goofy's Mini-Golf and costumed character appearances, a figure of Goofy hangs off the rear of the *Disney Magic* finishing painting the lettering.

Oceaneer Club and Lab

Disney's Oceaneer Club and Lab are the two clubs for kids ages three to 12 on all four Disney cruise ships. Trained youth staff will watch the children and lead them in a wide variety of activities.

On all Disney cruises, Oceaneer Lab and Oceaneer Club are now connected, so kids can move freely between activities. However, in general, Club activities appeal to the younger kids and Lab activities to older ones, though all kids in this age bracket are welcome at all activities.

Venues and activities vary by ship. Currently, *Disney Magic* features Andy's Room (from the Pixar animated film), Pixie Hollow (with Tinker Bell and her friends), Disney Junior play space (with elements from the television shows) and Marvel's Superhero Academy; *Disney Wonder* includes Andy's Room, Disney Junior play space, Marvel's Superhero Academy and the Oaken's Trading Post from *Frozen*; *Disney Dream* features Andy's Room, a Disney Infinity playspace, Pixie Hollow and a Millennium falcon-themed Star Wars play area with over 1,000 LED lights; and *Disney Fantasy* has Andy's Room, Pixie Hollow, a Star Wars Command Post with a holo-table, as well as a Doctor Strange space in its Marvel Superhero Academy.

Imagineer Joe Lanzisero described the Oceaneer Lab as a "mash-up of Jules Verne and Pirates of the Caribbean".

According to the back story on the *Disney Magic* and *Disney Wonder*, The *RV Oceaneer Lab* was the first ship of the fictitious S.E.A. (Society of Explorers and Adventurers) member Captain

Mary Oceaneer and the inspiration for the Oceaneer Club and Oceaneer Lab.

The *RV Oceaneer Lab's* maiden voyage took place on July 30, 1898 (referencing the *Disney Magic* debut in 1998). It served as Mary Oceaneer's floating base for her deep-sea diving excursions and treasure hunting expeditions.

Artifacts line the walls of the ship's public areas. These include a golden sword found on a deep sea dive on December 5, 1901 (with her parrot Salty's custom diving suit accompanying it) to a more recent expedition to Castaway Cay that yielded a variety of buried treasures.

Items relating to other members of S.E.A. like Henry Mystic and Harrison Hightower III are also on display. A scroll posted by a dagger on the wall proclaims: "Welcome to the Oceaneer Lab! I sincerely hope you enjoy the assemblage of artifacts, treasures and technologies gathered from ports of call all over the world. My top-notch crew will make your visit a memorable one. Captain Mary Oceaneer." At the bottom is a raised red seal of the S.E.A.

Some DCL Fatalities. People die every day, even on a Disney vacation cruise. The vast majority of deaths on cruise ships are natural, with most the result of heart attacks of older passengers.

Each cruise ship is required to carry body bags and maintain a small morgue room separate from food storage areas that can hold three bodies for no longer than a week with the body off-loaded at the next large port of call.

Of course, the Walt Disney Company does not want to publicize those who have accidents or die on one of their cruises but here are a few who were reported in local newspapers:

Rebecca Coriam a twenty-four year old UK citizen who worked on the *Disney Wonder* as a youth activities counselor disappeared March 22, 2011 and was presumed accidentally fallen overboard. No evidence of foul play was determined.

Phillip Munch, 56, from Tennessee passed away from natural causes in his cabin on March 1, 2015 while the ship was docked at Castaway Cay.

A 38-year-old-male passenger from the *Disney Wonder* was found February 26, 2015, drowned in the water of the adult beach at Castaway Cay. It was determined he had a pre-existing medical condition.

Richard Williams, 39, from Missouri, passed away of heart failure on June 15, 2015 on the *Disney Fantasy*.

Peter Mizioch, 75, from Arizona on September 12, 2015 on a cruise on the *Disney Fantasy* complained of dizziness and cold symptoms and was diagnosed as having positional vertigo. When the condition worsened later that day, he was flown from the Great Inagua Island to Broward Health Medical Center in Ft. Lauderdale where he passed away from cardiopulmonary arrest and hypertensive heart disease.

Austin Ray, 17, from Missouri was on a cruise with his parents aboard the *Disney Wonder* on May 31, 2016 when he suddenly stopped breathing. He had recently been diagnosed with Stage 4 kidney failure.

Lifeboat Drill. Regulations require every cruise to begin with a "muster drill". At approximately 4PM before the ship departs, the ship will sound its foghorn with the distress signal: seven blasts, followed by a longer eighth blast. Once that occurs, guests head to their muster station listed on their Key to the World Card and on the inside of their stateroom door that also shows the evacuation route.

Each stateroom is equipped with enough personal flotation devices (life jacket vests) for each person who is registered in the room. The vests are each equipped with water-triggered locator beacons, reflective identification, and whistles for attracting attention

All the muster stations are on the fourth deck where the rigid lifeboats are housed. There are also inflatable lifeboats that the guests don't see. During an emergency if a guest shows up without a life jacket, there are additional ones available at the muster station. Usually everyone shows up for the drill even if those who showed up promptly have to wait for stragglers or those who got lost.

Failure to show up results in an "invitation" during the cruise to attend a mandatory thirty minute class usually at the most inopportune time on the trip about the necessity of this activity and to review the information given to the guests who did show up. In 2019, Disney issued a pin only available on DCL ships of Mickey, Donald, Goofy and Pluto in their life jackets attending the drill.

The Art of the Ship

The Disney Cruise Line ships are floating art galleries boasting hundreds of pieces of artwork ranging from carefully selected prints to elaborate sculptures from stem to stern. That artwork directly honors the legacy of Walt Disney and the Walt Disney Company.

Throughout the ship, Walt's contribution to the art of animation is represented by rarely seen, authentic reproductions of artwork from the Disney vaults of story sketches, film stills and posters from the many classic Disney cartoons that had a nautical theme from *King Neptune* (1932) to *How To Be a Sailor* (1944) to *Alice's Day at Sea* (1923) that was the very first Disney Studio in Hollywood animated short ever made.

"There are so many surprises on the ship," stated Imagineer Joe Lanzisero. "You walk in and your jaw drops. Then you get down to the nuances of the materials and the craftsmanship. It is impossible to see it all but as Walt himself said, 'It's kind of fun to do the impossible'."

A Disney cruise costs at least twice as much as voyages on other cruise ships. In some cases, that additional cost is offset by amenities like limitless free soda and ice cream where other cruise lines charge for those items. Primarily, the extra cost is compensated by the Disney theming and detail throughout the ship, especially the artwork that is unique not only in its content but in its presentation.

Magic Portholes

Disney animation is alive and well on the Disney Cruise ships in an experience that is something unique to the *Disney Dream* and the *Disney Fantasy*.

Outside staterooms on a cruise have been prized because they have real windows and verandas to view the sea and moments like sunrises, sunsets and islands or other ships coming into view.

The "magic virtual portholes" in the interior rooms of the *Dream* and *Fantasy* are round 42 inch monitors showing the sea and outside activity in real time in the inside staterooms.

Bob Zalk, senior producer/director for WDI, explained that the live feed is accomplished with four HD cameras mounted around the ship: port, starboard, forward and aft. So wherever the inside stateroom is located—and there are about 150 on the ship or approximately 15 percent of the rooms—the virtual view will correspond exactly in real time.

To heighten that experience, there are approximately three-dozen different animation snippets that overlay the actual image. So, while watching the ocean, a guest might see the steamboat from *Steamboat Willie* (1928) chugging along or Wall-E and Eve flying by together above the water. There are supposedly a few different ones on the *Disney Fantasy* than on the *Disney Dream*.

"With the Disney animated library being what it is, there is no shortage of Disney characters and scenes and vignettes we can choose from," Zalk said. "The challenge sometimes for us is not what will we pick, but how do we whittle those picks down to the best."

This process is similar to the experience in the Finding Nemo Submarine Voyage attraction at Disneyland Park or the SeaCabs in the Living Seas with Finding Nemo pavilion at Epcot where guests can look into a real water environment, but see a brief animated segment interacting with the actual marine background.

A switch to the right of the bed can turn off the view above the bed plunging the room into complete darkness, as well.

Of course, Disney has never released a list of all of these animated segments, wanting guests to enjoy the joy of discovery. In fact, the segments run randomly (although, in general, you can expect to see one every 15 or so) and mix up the order so it isn't an established loop. You won't be able to determine that if you just saw a particular scene that you should stick around because the next scene is one of your favorites. It may turn out to be something else entirely unexpected.

Each segment lasts just a few seconds, some longer than others. Some feature a gag punch line at the end (often a character dropping into the water and creating a splash) while others just drift off. Many of the characters fly through either on their own or connected to something, like balloons.

There are segments of classical Disney animation, as well as Pixar films and even one featuring the Muppet Gonzo. Some animation was newly created, while other selections were obviously taken from the actual cartoons.

These clips are without sound so there is no audio warning that they are being shown. All in all, it is an impressive and clever job by Disney and is very entertaining. Imagineer Joe Lanzisero was the one who selected which segments would be animated from a proposal that featured dozens.

He said that he picked what he thought might be the most fun for guests and called it a "Disney differentiator," that is one of the things that makes a Disney Cruise different.

Here is a partial list that I have put together of the ones that I have seen on the *Disney Dream*:

- The Barrel of Red Monkeys from Pixar's *Toy Story* (1995) form a link chain from the top of the porthole screen to pull up Mr. Potato Head wearing a construction hat from the bottom.
- Mr. Potato Head pops upside down from the top of the porthole screen, loses his hat, waves and then loses his grip and falls to the bottom.
- Mr. Potato Head pops up slyly part way from the bottom right, top right, and bottom left before dashing off to the left.
- Mr. Potato Head holds up his eye from the bottom of the porthole to check things out and then pops up completely.
- The metal claw appears from the top of the porthole screen and drops down and pulls up three happy green aliens from *Toy Story* (1995) who wave.
- Woody from *Toy Story* desperately holds onto a huge out-of-control kite and flies around.

- Woody hanging on to the back of Buzz Lightyear from *Toy Story* flies around.
- Slinky Dog from *Toy Story* drops down from the top of the screen and then springs back up.
- A bunch of colorful balloons floats up from the bottom of the porthole and holding on to the strings is Kevin, the goofy bird from Paradise Falls in Pixar's *UP* (2009), who is hanging upside down and letting his head droop. Cleverly, Disney has also included three other variations featuring the exact same bunch of colorful balloons floating upwards from the bottom. In one variation, holding onto the strings is Carl Fredricksen, who drops his cane and, in another variation, it is the Russell in his scout uniform. There is also a version where Dug the dog is hanging underneath the balloons.
- In the distance, the house from *UP* drifts slowly across the horizon held up by balloons.
- Winnie the Pooh drops down from the top of the porthole screen hanging onto a green balloon and giggling.
- Winnie the Pooh desperately grabs on to Piglet's scarf as it unravels and he is buffeted around the sky since it seems to be a blustery day.
- Flit, the little green humming bird from *Pocahontas* (1995), zips back and forth and plunges into the sea and reappears soaked and then recovers and flies off.
- The blue spy car Finn McMissile and Tow Mater from *Cars 2* (2011) both drop down on ropes from the top of the porthole screen. When Mater's rope snaps and he drops into the ocean, Finn shoots a line to rescue him.
- Lightning McQueen from *Cars* (2006) leaps high in the air toward the porthole with his tongue hanging out.
- Peter Pegasus, the little black flying horse from *Fantasia* (1940) awkwardly flies around and then rejoins the rest of his family to fly away.
- Gonzo floats down from above as he is skydiving but eventually falls like a rock.
- Wall-E from the Pixar movie *Wall-E* (2008) zips in the air throughout the screen.

- The Cheshire Cat from *Alice in Wonderland* (1951) does a series of odd poses including losing his head.
- Pegasus, the white flying horse from *Hercules* (1997), playfully flies around.
- Flounder from *The Little Mermaid* (1989) leaps up and down in the sea and Scuttle the seagull flies by and scoops him up.
- Medieval Mickey and Minnie (wearing a princess cap) swing around on a corset back and forth from the short *Ye Olden Days* (1933) from the colorized version of that cartoon.
- A wonderful series of clips from *Plane Crazy* (1928) of Mickey and Minnie flying back and forth in Mickey's homemade airplane and then eventually crashing into the porthole.
- The three flying cherub cupids from *Fantasia* play their horns causing a dancing rainbow to appear and swirl up and down.
- Kaa the snake from *Jungle Book* (1967) drops down from the top of the screen and he smiles as his eyes start to swirl to hypnotize you, but Bagheera the panther's claw grabs the snake by the neck and pulls him up.
- Sir Hiss, the snake assistant to Prince John in *Robin Hood* (1973) has his head inside a pink balloon and he huffs and puffs to get some altitude and then uses his tail as a propeller to move around. A gust of wind blows him away. There is a variation to this scene as well. Sir Hiss floats around with his head in the balloon and the balloon pops and he drops straight down.
- Captain Hook from *Peter Pan* (1953) drops down from the top of the porthole screen clinging precariously by his hook over the sea where the crocodile leaps up and snaps at him.
- Jiminy Cricket from *Pinocchio* (1940) playfully hops up and down and eventually opens his umbrella and floats away.
- Princess Dot, the youngest daughter of the Queen in Pixar's *A Bug's Life* (1998), playfully flies around.
- Tinker Bell, Peter Pan, Wendy, Michael and John fly carefree around the sky from *Peter Pan*
- Tinker Bell flies into the scene and in an action reminiscent of the opening of the weekly Disney television show and flicks her wand to create a shower of pixie dust.

- Dumbo from *Dumbo* (1941) flies around holding his magic feather.
- A dozing Pluto floats by on a flying "Welcome" mat like a magic carpet and then is horrified to discover where he is.
- The lighted lanterns from *Tangled* (2010) fill the sky and float away.
- A smiling Rapunzel from *Tangled* swings by on her long hair.
- Peach, the starfish from *Finding Nemo* (2003) gets stuck to the center of the porthole, waves, looks around and then gleefully detaches.
- Archimedes, Merlin's owl in *The Sword in the Stone* (1963) and Wart (the young King Arthur transformed by Merlin's magic into a yellow-orangish sparrow) fly around the screen.
- Ray, the Cajun firefly from *Princess and the Frog* (2009), appears and, in an interesting twist, sky writes out the words "Sweet Dreams" in a puff of smoke at the end of his segment.
- Panchito and Jose Carioca from *The Three Caballeros* (1944) float by on their magic flying serape. They each hold spyglasses that they use to search for something or someone (perhaps Donald Duck?) even looking directly at you.
- Aladdin and Jasmine from *Aladdin* (1992) fly by on their magic carpet and smile and wave.
- Kronk and Yzma from *Emperor's New Groove* (2000) fly together in an odd contraption that gets hits by lightning incinerating it.
- Pacha and Kuzco from *Emperor's New Groove* climb up each side of the porthole back-to-back in a way reminiscent of a scene in the movie but eventually end up falling into the sea.
- Hyacinth Hippo from *Fantasia* (1940) in her tutu delicately skips across the surface of the water.
- Goofy, in a segment from the cartoon short *Hawaiian Holiday* (1937), blissfully sails across lying prone on his surfboard until it suddenly drops out from underneath him and he drops into the ocean.
- The band from *The Band Concert* (1935) cartoon short, including Mickey Mouse as the conductor, swirl through the sky as if caught in a tornando along with musical stands,

music sheets and more just like in the similar scene from the cartoon.
- The three fairies from *Sleeping Beauty* (1959), Flora, Fauna and Merryweather use their magic to create a pink lettered "Welcome" underneath them. After they fly off, Merryweather returns and with her wand changes the letters to the color blue.
- Colorful fireworks light up the sky (even in daytime) with the finally flurry forming three circles like a Mickey Mouse head silhouette.
- From *Tugboat Mickey* (1940) Mickey is on top of a mast using a brush to seal it when a nearby pelican swallows the open can of sealant.
- The large face of Stitch appears and his tongue licks the entire porthole leaving a slimy coating.
- One animated effect that kept occurring is a swirl of pixie dust that explodes in the middle of the screen just seconds before a segment appears. There is no character involved, just the effect, and I believe it is originally from the opening of the early version of the weekly Disney television show.

Enchanted Art

Primarily near elevators and staircases are pieces of "Enchanted Art" that seem to resemble artwork for animation cels, theatrical cartoon posters or vintage photos among other things.

If you ask the crew on the Disney Dream how these enchanted pieces of art spring magically to life, they will usually respond "Disney magic" just as when I was a cast member and guests asked about the line extending off Cinderella Castle I would reply, "Cinderella finally got cable" or "Peter Pan was afraid that Tinker Bell might get lost at night finding her way back to Neverland so drew a line in the sky."

The Enchanted Art pieces are LCD screens equipped with facial recognition sensors. If you look closely on the surrounding frame you will find the little white circle. One way of finding some of these experiences is to look for a bronze like circle with an icon of a magnifying glass on the floor in front of the picture since some of the pieces are used in the Midship Detective Agency game.

In addition to the 22 animated pictures of Enchanted Art, the *Disney Dream* features roughly 200 pieces of artwork that does not animate. These pieces often include reproductions of rarely seen model sheets and concept art.

Imagineer Joe Lanzisero stated, "The Enchanted Art pieces are scattered around the ship to surprise guests. It just happens before your eyes. You never think about what goes into it."

Vice president of entertainment Jim Urry added, "The idea is that guests will see one and then they'll start walking around the ship, trying to find others. But they might stand in front of another piece of art for five minutes before realizing it doesn't do anything."

In fact, some of the Enchanted Art is placed next to a nearby "regular" print to try to fool guests trying to figure out a pattern. The enchanted artwork doesn't glow like a regular computer screen or television and has a covering coated in an anti-glare finish to enable it to blend in with other artwork that is displayed.

Greg Butkus, concept designer principal for Walt Disney Imagineering, said:

> This type of storytelling helps make time on the ship unique and different from the Parks. Ultimately, we want to create a one-of-a-kind Disney experience.

No one, including the Disney Company, has posted a list of all the Enchanted Art on board or its location. So, while according to Disney part of the fun is discovering some of these pieces on your own, I am sharing several on the *Disney Dream* that I especially liked to get you started:

Deck 2 Midship, to the right of the entrance of the hallway to the Enchanted Garden restaurant, is what looks like a cel of young Bambi, Thumper and Flower playing with a butterfly.

Deck 3 near Guest Services, are two posters for the Silly Symphonies *Flowers and Trees* (1932) and *Birds in the Spring* (1933). With a little patience, you can see a flock of black birds fly from one poster to another and then back again.

Deck 3 by the Midship elevators on the port side toward the bar is a cel of Ben Ali Gator and Hyacinth Hippo from *Fantasia* (1940) doing three different dance routines.

Deck 4 Forward. Two of my favorite framed photos are outside the balcony entrances to the Walt Disney Theater.

One photo on the port side shows Walt sketching on a large piece of paper on a drawing easel and then the sketches come to life with brief animation from the first three Mickey Mouse cartoons: *Plane Crazy, Gallopin' Gaucho,* and *Steamboat Willie.*

Just a few feet away on the starboard side is another photo of Walt standing by a camera and the screen springs to life with short clips from three of his earliest black and white silent cartoons: *Alice in the Jungle* (1925), *Alice's Mysterious Mystery* (1926 and featuring a bit of animation of Julius the cat that mimics the distinctive walk of another silent cartoon star, Felix the Cat) and *Alice Gets in Dutch* (1924). Even the reel on the camera near Walt twirls as the clips are shown.

Deck 4 in the Skyline nightclub. A poster on the wall opposite the bar features an international image that changes when the screens above the bar change. For instance, the Italian poster has three Vespa scooters that will roar to life as the green, red and white colors of the Italian flag highlight them.

Deck 5 Aft by the elevators and stairs on the port side are two adjacent pictures of a pirate ship and an old fort. The two interact with the ship firing at the fort just like in the famous Disneyland theme park attraction, Pirates of the Caribbean. In fact, the sounds that are heard are taken directly from the soundtrack for that attraction.

Deck 5 One piece of art that adults can only view on the first day Open House of the Oceaneer Club and Lab features a portrait of Mr. Gibbs. Joshamee Gibbs, often just referred to as just "Mr. Gibbs" is a major character in the *Pirates of the Caribbean* film franchise appearing in all the films so far as well as videogames and books. He is Captain Jack Sparrow's longtime friend and frequent first mate. He is portrayed in the films by actor Kevin McNally.

The portrait is located to the back on the Oceaneer Lab on the Aft wall. The only movement is his lips but he says multiple phrases including "Time to hoist the Jolly Roger", "A pirate's life for me….and you and you and you….", "I'm setting a course for the poolside buffet. It's the cupcakes I'm after", "Remember the pirate code, no swimming without your floaties", "We never had no water slide" and "Welcome aboard, me buckos" as well as many others.

Deck 5 Midship port. A Map of the Caribbean by the cruise excursion desk. Over a dozen vintage things spring to life:
- A red crab scuttles across the Tropic of Cancer line.
- A jelly fish swims by in the upper left while there is a pirate ship on the right.
- A green sea monster appears and jumps over the Dominican Republic.
- A green turtle swims slowly near the bottom.
- A diver's helmet pops up with an eye in it.
- Jumping dolphins flip in and out of the water near Cuba and later the Dominican Republic.
- A pirate ship is in a sea battle with another ship and a cannon ball sinks that ship.
- A Chinese junk ship sails through the waters and a huge green fish snaps it up.
- A hammerhead shark swims around.
- A purple sea monster pops up.
- A colorful parrot flies through the picture.
- A green sea monster (whose head reminded me of Gorgo) appears and waves.

Deck 5 Midship starboard. Turning Captain Hook steering wheel allows the guest to maneuver the Jolly Roger around the Neverland Lagoon on the quest for treasure among other things while intriguing obstacles like the snapping crocodile appear and the ship needs to be sprinkled by Tinker Bell to fly over it.

Deck 6 Forward by elevators. Three scenes inspired by the cartoon *Boat Builders* (1938) with Mickey, Donald and Goofy looking at plans and building a boat. They build three boats: S.S. Goofy, S.S. Minnie and S.S. Daisy all with disastrous results.

Deck 7 Aft by the elevators and stairs is what looks like a cel from the Mickey Mouse cartoon *Hawaiian Holiday* (1937) that was made roughly 22 years before Hawaii became an official state. It was inspired by Walt's Hawaiian vacation trip to Oahu in 1934 where he tried to learn how to surf with not much success that is parodied by Goofy's attempts in the cartoon. It is only one of four cartoons featuring the Fab Five (Mickey, Minnie, Donald,

Goofy, Pluto) made while Walt was alive. Donald dances in a grass skirt that catches fire. Minnie dances in a hula skirt while Mickey plays the slide guitar. Goofy surfs atop some waves.

Deck 8 Forward Elevators. Port (These poster images change each day).

- Poster promoting DCL Alaska cruise with Mickey in a lumberjack outfit laying on the wing of a totem pole figure, the totem pole faces move, the DCL ship leaves and returns, birds fly by and ice floes move, fish jump.
- Poster with Minnie in a beach chair on Castaway Cay. Butterflies move.
- Poster promoting Mexico cruise with Senorita Minnie where the moon rises and sets, white doves fly and more.

Deck 8 Forward Elevators. Starboard (These poster images change each day).

- Poster promoting the tropical lagoons of the Mexican Rivera. Goofy is scuba diving and he tickles the chin of a purple fish, ship horn sounds and shakes up Goofy so that his mask fills with water and spouts out his breathing tube
- Poster promoting Castaway Cay with Donald Duck parasailing and Huey, Dewey and Louie in a kayak.
- Poster of Nassau with Goofy in an inner tube where he snores and zips around in the tube, Pluto pops up, jumping fish.

Deck 9 Aft Elevators Alice in Wonderland floats down the rabbit hole. She gets a cup of tea, then the Mad Hatter refills her cup and finally she passes by a mirror where she is upside down and she sees the smiling Cheshire Cat in the mirror.

Deck 10 Forward Elevators Ursula the sea witch conjures up two lost souls she has claimed; Ariel plays with red underwater flowers and seahorses come out; an octopus is surrounded by dancing lobsters and seahorses.

Deck 11 Cove Café on wall to the left of the bar. Walt standing on the beach in Rio in South America with Sugarloaf mountain in the background. The man on the left is animator Frank Thomas and the man on the right is storyman Jim Bodero. They were all there gathering material for the film that would become *Saludos*

Amigos (1942). Panchito and Jose ride a flying serape between Walt and the two other men and in one scene look at the viewer with telescopes.

Deck 13 Aft inside by door leading to the mini-golf course. Goofy is at a tee and lifting his club to swing and he twists his entire body several times and when it untwists he flies off like a helicopter; he swings his club and loses his grip so it whirls in the air like a boomerang and smashes him on the back of his head; he swings at golf ball and it goes down his vest tickling him and then through his pants and into the hole.

The Enchanted Art will only come to life if it senses that someone is not just casually glancing but pausing to look. A small camera sensor hidden in the frame detects that look and launches into a five-to-30-second piece of animation. Touching the artwork will not activate it. Listen closely since the movement is also accompanied by appropriate sound.

In general, there are three different animated sequence variations if you stand there long enough. Amazingly, Disney is currently working on updating the technology so the facial recognition will enable the artwork to know you have already seen it and what animation you have and have not seen.

The WDI spokesperson for the Enchanted Art is Estefania "Stef" Pickens, associate interactive show producer for Disney Imagineering stated:

> They look just like just another painting on the wall but they [the paintings] can recognize that you are there and trigger something special for you. It's definitely unique.

The idea started with the Magic Mirrors in place at Disney stores. But Imagineers took that basic concept a big step first with interactive adventures at Walt Disney World like the Sorcerers of the Magic Kingdom.

Pickens continued:

> A large team, which includes animators, directors, producers and technicians, is behind the creation of the Dream's interactive art. Themes had to be chosen, animation sequences developed — even the frames were a problem to be solved, as they needed to be attractive, while at the same time hide the technical components.

WDI Principal Concept Designer Greg Butkus explained:

It's storytelling with technology. It gives you a deeper level of immersion.

Imagineer Diego Parras added:

We use cutting-edge technology all the time. But we really have to make sure that technology is invisible. At the end of the day our guests just want to be entertained. We want them to say, "Wow, that's Crush talking to us while we're having dinner."

While all of this is very impressive, thirteen pieces of Enchanted Art around the Disney Dream serves an additional function. They are used for two family oriented hunt games connected with the Midship Detective Agency. For these pictures, usually there is a circular metal shape on the floor in front of them with a magnifying glass.

There is a "rule of three" in animation. For instance, in terms of an animation gag, a good gag is done three times: first in its original form to get a laugh, then repeated later to get a laugh of recognition that the audience knows what is going to happen before the characters do, and then finally done again but with a twist at the end to get a laugh of surprise that it was different than expected.

Something that most people who discover a piece of Enchanted Art never realize is that each piece has three different variations and they walk away after just seeing one of the versions.

For instance on Deck 2 on the Port (left) side near the entrance to the Enchanted Garden restaurant, there is what looks like a painted cel from the classic Disney animated feature, *Bambi* (1942).

Thumper the Rabbit is on a tree log looking at the young Bambi. One version has a butterfly land on Bambi's nose making Thumper laugh so hard he rocks backward. Another version has the butterfly fly off of Bambi's nose and tickle Thumper's tummy and then land on Bambi's tail. The third version has Flower the skunk pop up from the underbrush while Bambi blows off the butterfly from his tail and it ends up on Flower's nose. (A laughing Flower falls back into the underbrush at the start of the next scene.)

Some of the art is actually programmed to interact with a piece next to it. I was disappointed in a recent sailing on the *Disney Dream* to see that the Vista Gallery had been replaced by Tiffany & Company store because it removed one of my favorite Enchanted Art pieces that was not relocated anywhere else on ship that I could find.

In the Vista Gallery on Deck 4 selling artwork (including some nice pieces done by my friends Alex Maher and Don "Ducky" Williams), there was one painting that was not for sale. It was the "Minnie Lisa" (a parody of the famous Mona Lisa painting featuring Minnie Mouse by artist Maggie Parr). Minnie blinks and birds start chirping in the sky and Tinker Bell whizzes across the painting among other things if you were patient.

I believe the painting may still exist on the *Disney Fantasy* along with another Parr painting of "Pinkie Daisy" featuring Daisy Duck inspired by Thomas Lawrence's famous painting "Sarah Barrett Moulton: Pinkie."

Some other examples on the *Disney Fantasy* include: Dual circus art posters featuring Dumbo and Timothy Q. Mouse flying from one frame into the other, Walt Disney animating three new clips that spring from his sketch pad, featuring the Fab Five: Mickey, Minnie, Goofy, Donald and Pluto., Scenes from Disney's classic animated film *Fantasia* depicting dancing fairies set to "Nutcracker Suite" and a frolicking unicorn and satyr set to "The Pastoral Symphony", and fanciful animations of "Alice in Wonderland" inspired by Disney Legend Mary Blair's artwork.

The Midship Detective Agency

The Midship Detective Agency on the *Disney Dream* and the *Disney Fantasy* cruise ships is the latest evolution in a series of interactive games that were first available at Walt Disney World.

Kim Possible World Showcase Adventure had guests using customized cellphones (Kimmunicators that were actually a Motorola i870 phone programmed for the game) to receive clues and directions around World Showcase (Mexico, Norway, China, Germany, Japan, France, and United Kingdom) at Epcot to help Kim Possible and Ron Stoppable. The beta test was held in 2006 with the final version debuting in 2009 and lasting until May 2012.

In June 2012, the experience was replaced by Agent P's (the alter ego of Phineas and Ferb's pet platypus Perry) World Showcase Adventure that required guests to sign up and be issued an official FONE (Field Operative Notification Equipment) or their own smartphone to connect with Major Monogram and his intern Carl to get a series of clues. Up to four guests could join forces to stop Dr. Doofenshmirtz from wreaking havoc. There are seven different adventures (China, France, Germany, Italy, Japan, Mexico, and United Kingdom pavilions). That version ended in 2019 to be replaced with a newer version using characters from the animated *DuckTales* series.

A version called Sorcerers of the Magic Kingdom using cards debuted at the Magic Kingdom in February 2012 where Merlin is recruiting apprentice sorcerers to defeat Hades and his fellow villains, Yzma, Cruella, Scar, Jafar, Maleficent, Ursula, Ratcliffe, and Dr. Facilier, who are searching for four shards to create a magic crystal.

There are nine quests and the guest is given a map, a Sorcerer Key Card, five spell cards, and brief training to find the 20 magic portals scattered throughout the various lands (except Tomorrowland). Merlin appears in the final portal welcoming the guest to the rank of Master Sorcerer.

Using the same technology developed for these other interactive activities that utilized screens that looked like windows, Midship Detective Agency had its soft opening on March 6, 2012, as part of the preview cruises. It opened to the general public on March 31, 2012, when the *Disney Dream* embarked on its maiden voyage.

The Midship Detective Agency (located in kiosks on Deck 5) enables guests to grab a square "detective badge" and a casebook (that includes a map for the specific Enchanted Art needed to be used).

The badge is actually a card that looks like an ordinary playing card but is printed with a unique 2-D barcode icon on one side. When you hold the "detective badge" up to the Enchanted Art you discover it functions like a wireless game controller.

Holding the card up to a specified piece of artwork triggers an animated activity (like moving the card to unscrew bolts from a wall or moving the light of a flashlight around to locate something) that needs to be done in order to discover the lost painting or rescue one of the Dalmatian puppies from the animated feature *101 Dalmatians*. It may take a little practice to properly manipulate the card in connection with the artwork.

The Imagineers designed the game so it can be played at an individual's own pace including the ability to start and stop at any time. On average, it has been determined that the game takes 25 to 45 minutes to complete.

The Imagineers even included an added level that will bring a smile to the face of adults including that the missing paintings game having paintings where Goofy is inserted into the classic "Washington Crossing the Delaware" and Minnie Mouse poses in Botticelli's "The Birth of Venus."

The attraction follows a format similar to Sorcerers of the Magic Kingdom in that a card, rather than a phone, is used. The card activates different Enchanted Art locations in finding clues and missing items. They have a special fold-out pamphlet with a map of the location of the art, a place for notes, profiles of the suspects and the hint that "you won't need to visit every location to solve the case".

This unique barcode, which is activated at one of the self-service kiosks, keeps track of which crime you selected to solve and your progress during your cruise. The game card remembers where you have been and what clues you have discovered.

The seven suspects are Jafar, Maleficent, The Evil Queen (from Snow White), Captain Hook, Dr. Facilier, Yzma, and Cruella De Vil. With several potential villains, guests can play several times without repeating a case because it rotates so that a different villain is the culprit needing to be caught.

- **The Case of the Plundered Paintings**: There are missing paintings and the detectives need to recover them and identify the culprit. Every play-through has a different culprit.
- **The Case of the Missing Puppies**: Roger Radcliffe and Pongo need help to find the missing 99 puppies from *101 Dalmatians*. It's not Cruella, the most obvious suspect. Detectives find she is not even on the ship.
- **The Case of the Stolen Show**: The Muppets (20 of them) are prepared to start production for a show on the ship but the props have disappeared so Kermit the Frog goes to Mickey's Midship Detective Agency office to get help. However, inside the office is Pepe the King Prawn who is temporarily taking over while Mickey is out to lunch. (Mickey makes a voice-over cameo at the end of the game finding that someone has changed the locks to his office.) For this crime, the real suspects are Fozzie Bear, Camilla (Gonzo's chicken girlfriend), Beauregard, Bobo the Bear, Lew Zealand, and Rizzo the Rat. The Muppet footage was directed by Kirk Thatcher.

In the rush to get on the job of solving the crime, guests often miss the nice details at the two sign-in desks on Midship Deck 2 and 5 that are filled with various clippings. For future researchers (and those who put together ship scavenger hunts for their group) here is what is displayed on the two desks.

Deck 5 Midship Detective Agency Desk

Newspaper Clipping:

Cruise News Vol. III No. DCLXXXVII
All The News Afloat Special Edition 8 cents
Extra! Extra! Crimes at Sea!

Midship Detective Agency Chief Detective Mickey Mouse reports that some really big cases have just come across his desk aboard the Disney Dream. "These are some doozy cases!" said Mickey who reports that he needs the help of new detectives right away! Founded in 2011, the Midship Detective Agency is the *Disney Dream's* newest addition.

Newspaper Ad: "Jan. 26 Midship Detective Agency opens today. "No ship too big, no case too small. If you need help, just call." (Echoing the theme song of the syndicated television show *Chip'n'Dale's Rescue Rangers*.)

Note:

From the Desk of Goofy.

"Dear Mickey, Gwarsh! Still working on that case of the missing sock! The dryer is my main suspect. Kind regards, Goofy."

Telegram:

To: Mickey Mouse Midship Detective Agency. From: The ship's cruise director.

"Thank you for locating my hat. Who knew I was wearing it the entire time except for you. Brilliant job! You make our ship proud. Now where are my glasses? Oh, wait, here they are."

Newspaper Clipping:

Pete causes havoc being mean and despicable aboard the *Disney Dream*. Pete vows: "You'll never catch me, Mickey Mouse." Jan. 27

List (comments by Pepe the King Prawn in parentheses):

How To Be an Ace Detective (Pepe's notes to self)

- Carry a Magnifying glass. (Next time, remember glass)

- Compile List of Suspects
- Study Every Clue. (Sure, why not? Okay.)
- Carry a Casebook and write things down (Find an assistant to do most of the work.)
- Wear a Fedora (Yes, ladies love it.)

Deck 2 Midship Detective Agency Desk

Telegram:

To: Mickey Mouse Midship Detective Agency
From: The ship's captain

"Mickey, congratulations on catching Pete! That despicable villain stole my dress whites and tried to dye them a different color. But you caught him red handed! Now I can still go to the formal dinner tonight. I am in your debt."

Newspaper Clipping:

Captain honors Mickey Mouse for catching Pete! Pete declares, "I guess I should never have said never." Jan. 29

Wanted Poster:

Pete. Wanted for: Being mean and despicable. Aliases: Peg-Leg Pete, Bad Pete, Mighty Pete, Pete the Cat. (A red stamp saying "Caught" over Pete's picture.)

The Muppet Call Board

On Deck 4 forward port (left) there is a Muppet Call Board for the supposed show the Muppets are producing just outside the Walt Disney Theater. If you choose "The Case of the Stolen Show" at the Midship Detective Agency, you will be directed to find this board.

Here are some of the items posted on that board:

- A Midship Detective Agency badge modified to showcase Pepe the King Prawn and identify it as his detective agency. Below is a posting with tear-away slips (some of which are missing) that states: "Come visit MY detective agency. Help me solve the case, ok?....so I can take credit."
- Button: "It's not easy bein' green".
- Poster: "This egg-citing act is definitely for the birds! 'Poultry in Motion' starring Camilla".
- Poster: "Rowlf plays songs in the key of Woof"

THE ART OF THE SHIP 99

- Poster: "The ABCs because 'ABC" spells 'Fun'!" The ABCs are Animal, Beaker and Chef (Swedish Chef).
- Poster: "See Gonzo the Great in his hottest performance ever with the amazing AquaDuck".
- Poster: "The Muppets Present 'Goin' Overboard'."
- Notice: "Costume Pick Up. 'Rhapsody in Red'. Red sequined vest, pants, bow tie."
- Notice: "Set Painting Duty for 'Bein' Green' set. Brushes provided with lots of green paint."

Disney Dream Elevator Art

The Midship elevators on the *Disney Dream* with their clear sides facing the Atrium offer a fascinating view of the lobby. However, what happens when that clear view is blocked after Deck 5 as the elevator continues to ascend?

Well, there are painted images of Disney animated characters who are also ascending or descending, depending upon your point of view.

On the port (left) side elevator:

- Mickey Mouse and Goofy are in a homemade helicopter. Mickey is sitting comfortably sipping pink lemonade and wearing sunglasses. Goofy wears flight goggles and is pedaling.
- Donald Duck is floating in a deck chair attached to a red and yellow checkered balloon. There is a wild looking bird (not the Aracuan) sitting on top of the balloon.
- Elastigirl from *The Incredibles* is in the form of a parachute as she holds on to her children: Dash and Violet.
- Dumbo (with Timothy the Mouse in his hat) happily flies in the air while being fed from a bag of peanuts by the crows from the movie.
- The three *Sleeping Beauty* fairies (Flora, Fauna and Merryweather) chase after Maleficient's black raven Diablo turning him blue and red.
- The floating house from Pixar's *UP* (2009) has both Carl and Dug, the talking dog, hanging onto a rope.

On the starboard (right) side elevator:
- There is a black and white picture of Mickey and Minnie kissing in the plane from *Plane Crazy* (1928) with heart-shaped white exhaust.
- Zazu the hornbill and Timon the meerkat from *The Lion King* (1994) battle over a screaming green worm who is in both their clutches and is being stretched.
- Tinker Bell is in the air sprinkling pixie dust on the nurse-maid dog Nana and little Michael Darling clutching his teddy bear who also floats in the air.
- Jasmine and Aladdin are bouncing atop the magic carpet they are riding and the turbulence is caused by the Genie underneath blowing upwards on the carpet.
- The Three Caballeros (Donald Duck, Jose Caricoa and Panchito) are riding on a magic serape. Jose and Panchito are playing on guitars but Donald is reaching down to try to grab his fallen guitar that has somehow fallen into the clutches of 10 baby Panchitoes who are singing and playing.
- Woody from *Toy Story* (1995) desperately holds on to the flying Buzz Lightyear but in the process Woody loses his boots and hat.

Jolly Roger Steering Wheel

On the *Disney Dream* on the starboard (right) side on Deck 5 atrium and near the entrance to the Bibbidi Bobbidi Boutique is a steering wheel for Captain Hook's pirate ship, the *Jolly Roger*. In front of the wheel is an Enchanted Art painting of the Neverland Lagoon.

Turn the wheel and animation in the picture allows you to maneuver Hook's ship around the cove. Your goal is to move the ship to touch the glowing treasure that is on the edge of the shore. Once you touch it, it will spring into the ship and you have completed that scene. As with the other Enchanted Art pictures, there are three variations (including treasure inside a giant clam shell over toward the right hand side).

Making the ship match your steering the wheel is harder than you might imagine (and my lack of coordination often got the ship "stuck" on the shore which requires some finesse to get back moving in the water) and to make it more difficult, one scene introduces the snapping crocodile (retroactively named officially Tick-Tock by Disney) from the animated *Peter Pan* feature popping up out of the water to block your progress. If you attempt to go around the menacing reptile, he merely pops back up in your new path. I can see why Captain Hook got frustrated by the persistent creature.

I found that I had to bump into Tinker Bell (who doesn't appear on any regular schedule) who would then pixie dust the entire ship and it would glow and briefly fly and if you were clever enough you could fly over the crocodile to get to the treasure. I know because I did it more than once but was unable to do it with any consistency.

There's even an authentic-looking brass throttle lever on the left-hand side that you can use to control speed. Pushing it forward slightly speeds up the ship.

Despite spending quite some time at the wheel, there were other things that I still have not figured out. At one point, there were people on the left-hand side moving toward the pier. Was I supposed to go pick them up? Tiki torches started to flicker. Was I supposed to go toward them to trigger some new effect?

At one point, the eyes of Skull Rock started to glow red and there was also a red star in the sky. What does that all mean? Were they beckoning me to do something or were they sparked to life by something I had unintentionally done? Another guest told me they saw a rainbow appear, but I never did.

Transportation Paintings

On the *Disney Dream* on Deck 5 Midship port (left) there are a series of paintings on the wall depicting different types of transportation, and I have no idea why they are there, but they are done in a stylized form befitting the art from the Golden Age of Cruising. I bet many people never see them on their entire voyage. From left to right, they are:

- Casey Jr., the train from *Dumbo* (1942)
- Mickey's plane from *Plane Crazy* (1928)
- Cruella De Vil's distinctive car from 101 Dalmatians (1961)
- The ship *Queen Minnie* from the animated short cartoon *Boat Builders* (1938)

Also at the same location on the wall on the Aft side, before going down the hallway to the Oceaneer's Club are several brass plaques with raised images of Disney ships, but no identification. Moving left to right:

- Prince Eric's ship from *The Little Mermaid*
- The Jolly Roger from *Peter Pan*
- The Black Pearl from *Pirates of the Caribbean*
- The Flying Dutchman from *Pirates of the Caribbean*
- Mickey at the helm of the steamboat from *Steamboat Willie*

Disney Nautical Cartoons

The following are some of the nautical animated cartoons produced during Walt Disney's lifetime and are depicted in some of the framed art on the ships. Other non-maritime Disney cartoons are also in the art including *Alice in Wonderland, Bambi, Fantasia, Flowers and Trees* and more. Strangely, none of the following cartoons are shown on any channel on the stateroom televisions.

Alice's Day at Sea (1924) Alice goes to the seashore and falls asleep in a rowboat and dreams she is in a cartoon world under the sea.

Steamboat Willie (1928) The first theatrically released Mickey Mouse cartoon featuring Mickey as a mischievous deckhand on a riverboat run by Captain Pete.

Wild Waves (1929) Mickey and Minnie's day at the beach runs into trouble when Minnie is swept out to sea and Mickey must save her.

Frolicking Fish (1930) A Silly Symphony underwater musical with sea horses, lobsters, starfish and a villainous octopus.

The Beach Party (1931) Mickey and the gang find their fun at the seashore interrupted by a disgruntled octopus.

King Neptune (1932) Pirates capture a mermaid and all the underwater denizens go to her rescue including King Neptune stirring up a storm at sea.

Shanghaied (1934) Mickey saves Minnie from Peg Leg Pete's ship including using a stuffed swordfish in a frantic battle in the cabin.

Water Babies (1935) Loosely based on Charles Kingsley's story, a series of incidents with water nymphs riding on frogs and sailing lily pad boats.

Hawaiian Holiday (1937) On a beach in Hawaii, Minnie dances the hula accompanied by Mickey on a guitar, Pluto battles a starfish and Goofy attempts to surf.

Boat Builders (1938) Mickey, Donald and Goofy purchase a folding boat kit but it proves to be more difficult to put together than expected. After the *Queen Minnie* (a parody of the *Queen Mary* cruise ship) is finally christened, it promptly collapses.

The Whalers (1938) Mickey, Goofy and Donald are on a whaling ship but their encounter with a sleeping whale proves to be nothing but trouble for the trio.

Merbabies (1938) The redheaded young offspring of mermaids and mermen materialize out of the crashing surf and attend an underwater circus.

Beach Picnic (1939) Donald Duck teases Pluto at the beach with an inflatable rubber horse toy named Seabiscuit.

Sea Scouts (1939) Donald Duck in an Admiral's hat is continually frustrated by his three nephews who are his crew especially when they encounter a shark.

Tugboat Mickey (1940) Mickey is the captain of a tugboat with Donald and Goofy as his crew. When they attempt to answer a distress call, they accidentally blow up the ship and discover the call was just part of a radio drama.

How to Swim (1942) Goofy demonstrates diving and swimming techniques.

How to Be a Sailor (1944) Goofy demonstrates nautical knowledge from the first prehistoric use of floating logs to modern battleships including methods of navigation.

Sea Salts (1949) Bootle Beetle reminisces about his relationship with Donald Duck including the time they were shipwrecked.

Hello Aloha (1952) An overworked Goofy decides to quit his job and move to a carefree life on a South Pacific island.

Aquamania (1961) Goofy tries to impress his son with his water-skiing but inadvertently ends up in a championship race fraught with perils including an octopus and a roller coaster.

SEAcrets of DCL Art

Atrium Art: On the *Disney Magic* and the *Disney Wonder*, the bronze friezes that surround the atrium area on Decks 3 and 4 have Disney characters in costumes and doing things that the ship's crew would do.

On the *Disney Dream* and the *Disney Fantasy*, those bronze friezes show the characters attired in costuming and doing activities that the guests would do.

Daisy Duck is relaxing and reading a book in a deck chair at Serenity Bay, the adult beach on Castaway Cay. Donald Duck has snorkel gear and an inner tube for water activity at the family beach at Castaway Cay. Chip 'n' Dale are in sunglasses holding a life preserver and inflatable raft to enjoy some water fun. Mickey Mouse and Minnie are dressed elegantly and holding hands to enjoy Palo's or Remy's upscale restaurants.

Huey and Dewey with a spyglass are looking at a treasure map while Louie in a pirate captain's hat and swinging on a rope are celebrating Pirate's Night on the ship. Goofy and his son Max have golf clubs as they prepare to enjoy mini-golf on the Sports Deck 13 Aft.

The railing of the staircase has silhouette outline images of the faces of Mickey, Minnie, Goofy, Pluto and Donald.

Cinderella Mural: Two panels of the famous Dorothea Redmond designed mosaic mural in the breezeway of Cinderella's Castle at Walt Disney World have been recreated in part on Deck 3 Midship near Guest Services on the *Disney Dream*.

As many fans know the two ugly stepsisters have red and green faces to symbolize anger and envy while the two courtiers are caricatures of Disney Imagineers Herb Ryman (putting on Cinderella's slipper) and John Hench (with the beard). There is even an elegant throne chair in front of the mural for a photo opportunity.

DCL Dining

According to the Disney Cruise Line, on average during seven days at sea, the following food items are consumed:
- Beef—5,000 pounds
- Chicken—10,000 pounds
- Salmon—1,200 pounds
- Shrimp—1,300 pounds
- Lobster Tail—1,000 pounds
- Melon—15,000 pounds
- Pineapple—4,500 pounds
- Eggs—71,500
- Coffee—57,820 cups
- Soda—3,125 gallons
- Beer—12,385 bottles/cans
- Wine and Champagne—2,700 bottles

Some guests choose to sometimes avoid the regular dining restaurant rotation of the three main dining rooms and survive on room service, the quick serve locations that offer hamburgers, chicken tenders, pizza, fresh fruit, salads, and sandwich wraps among other items, the Cabanas buffet or even one of the two upscale restaurants that require special reservations and a significant up-charge.

The ships serve approximately 10,000 to 15,000 full meals every day. The galleys onboard use a Hobart dishwasher. No food is carried over from one seating to the next. All leftovers and unused meals are discarded after each seating. The galley is thoroughly cleaned and sanitized after each meal as well.

Each of the table service restaurants offers options to those who need gluten-free, vegetarian, no sugar added and dairy free options. If you request it in advance, you can also get kosher meals or other meal options.

Here is a brief look at some of the storytelling elements in some of the dining venues.

Disney Dream Main Dining Rooms

President of Disney Cruise Line in 1998 Art Rodney wanted something different in shipboard dining and came up with the rotating dining alternative. The principle was that when someone visits a city for the first time, the person normally tries a new restaurant each evening.

Rodney felt guests would appreciate that same experience at sea so DCL established three main dining rooms that were different in theme and menu and both the guests and their server staff would travel together to each during the voyage. In this way, the server staff could learn the preferences of the individual guests and anticipate those every night.

There are two seatings each evening and on cruises of four nights or longer, guess will repeat at least one of the same restaurants although the menus will change. At least one of these main dining rooms is also open for breakfast and lunch each day.

Animator's Palate

"Animation, and the art and techniques that create it, will always be the heart of Disney culture," said Imagineeer Joe Lanzisero.

The name Animator's Palate was intended as wordplay to suggest two very different things that sound the same.

An artist's palette is the surface used to squeeze out and mix paint. Traditionally, it was an oval wooden board with a hole for the thumb, so that artists could hold it while painting.

The word "palate" refers to taste. Someone who can taste slight nuances in food is said to have a well-developed palate or a sophisticated palate. Sometimes the taste of something is so strong that a palate should be cleansed to appreciate the subtle flavors of the next offering.

So Animator's Palate references not only a tool used in art but a tool used in tasting food.

Each DCL ship has a restaurant called Animator's Palate and each is meant to be a tribute to Disney animation. It has been determined both on the ships and in the theme parks that newer generations are more familiar with Pixar films and characters than the classic animated films so those elements are fairly prominent. However, there are three different versions of shows at these locations.

On the *Magic* and *Wonder*, since their first voyage, the restaurant is done up like a black-and-white sketchbook that magically transforms into full color during the meal.

This magic was originally accomplished by two parallel walls. The front wall has artwork in black and white while a second wall inches behind it has the same artwork in full color. At the beginning, the front wall is lighted so only the black and white can be seen. The wall was also perforated with small almost indistinguishable holes. During the evening, the light dims on the front wall and the back light on the color wall behind it is turned on and the color seems to seep through into the drawings.

The serving staff starts off the meal in vests with black-and-white artwork but they are reversible and out of sight of the diners they change them over so the same artwork is now in full color.

With technical upgrades to increase the sight and sound quality, this show is now called "Drawn to Magic" and is not offered on the *Dream* or *Fantasy*.

Over-sized digital canvases line the walls of the restaurant where unseen artists sketch character portraits that evolve into pencil tests of Disney characters and iconic moments from Disney animated films like *Beauty and the Beast, The Princess and the Frog* and more one canvas at a time. These pencil tests transform into full color when they are inked and painted.

There is a loose storyline of a hero's journey through Disney and Pixar animation from wishing upon a star to happily ever after with the canvases telling the story of dreams, featuring iconic wishing moments from films like *Tangled, The Princess and the Frog, Aladdin, Sleeping Beauty* as well as a confrontation with Disney villains.

The arrival of the Blue Fairy from the classic feature film *Pinocchio*, brings hope and a dash of magic imparting a rich splash of color to the walls of Animator's Palate climaxed by a parade of servers led by Sorcerer Mickey wending through the tables.

Set to an eloquent score composed by Randy Miller, and recorded at Capitol Studios in Hollywood, California, this show features music and animation from popular Disney movies that range from Disney's classic *Snow White* and the Seven Dwarfs, to the more contemporary films including *Wreck-It Ralph, Frozen, Big Hero 6, Zootopia, Finding Dory,* and *Moana*

On the *Dream* and *Fantasy*, Animator's Palate seeks to create the impression of a Disney animation studio and the process of producing animation with the use of character sketches, model sheets, story concept drawings, storyboards, film reels, maquettes (three-dimensional character models), paintbrushes, colored pencils, film strips and other tools associated with the business.

Shelves along the walls hold items that might be in an animator's room and the entire restaurant is vividly colorful. The backs of the dining room chairs are patterned after Mickey Mouse's pants, with red backs, yellow buttons and a black stripe of color across the top. Some video screens show short presentations on how animation is drawn.

There are fiber optic paint brush pillars and pencil columns. The ceiling is meant to resemble artist palettes and during the course of the evening colors seem to travel up the brushes and activate the vibrant colors in the palettes.

During the meal, the screens will switch to an undersea "Window to the Ocean" environment featuring the characters from *Finding Nemo* in a show called "Undersea Magic" that includes a one hour encounter with Crush the turtle as well as appearances of Nemo, Marlin, Dori, Bruce, Anchor, Chum, Mr. Ray, the moonfish and the gang from the tank. .

One hundred twenty-nine LCD monitors are placed throughout the room's nine "show zones," which are almost alcove-like and provide a more intimate dining experience.

Turtle Talk with Crush is a popular theater show that is part of Disney's Living Character Initiative program.

Bruce Vaughn, Vice President of Walt Disney Imagineering's Research and Development Division said, "This is an incredibly compelling and powerful way to experience the characters. They are fully aware of the people in their presence and can call you by name. It is a 100 percent live experience."

Crush is a laid-back green sea turtle over 150 years old who loves riding the ocean currents and talks with the stereotypical attitude and vocabulary of a California surfer. He first appeared in the Disney Pixar animated feature film *Finding Nemo* (2003) where he helped Dory and Marlin on their quest to find Marlin's son.

According to Crush himself, his father is named Mr. Turtle, so that would make Crush's full name Crush Turtle, or C. Turtle (sea turtle) for short. In the film, his voice is supplied by Nemo writer-director Andrew Stanton who recorded all of Crush's dialog lying on his couch in his office.

The show is a mixture of technologies including computer graphic techniques, image projection, digital puppetry and improvisation. Some of the action is pre-created animated sequences that can be cued up when needed while some of the action is done in real time.

Crush is controlled onscreen in real time by a puppeteer who uses a telemetric input device similar to a keyboard so that it appears seamlessly in a virtual environment. The X-Y-Z axis movement of the input device causes the digital puppet to move correspondingly.

Basically, a talented performer behind the massive rear projection screen area that looks like a window in to the Pacific Ocean underwater environment speaks in an approximation of Crush's familiar voice and it is transferred to the speakers in the small theater.

The avatar image is projected at 60 frames per second, so that the turtle's mouth is perfectly synchronized with the performer's words. The performance is a mixture of pre-scripted material and improvisational responses. Cameras mounted on either side of the screen, allows the performer to see the audience and to make specific references.

"Turtle Talk with Crush" originally opened on November 16, 2004 at The Living Seas pavilion at Epcot that was later renamed The Seas with Nemo and Friends. Another version opened at Disney California Adventure in July 2005. It was open briefly at Hong Kong Disneyland from May 24 to August 10, 2008. The attraction opened in Tokyo DisneySea on October 1, 2009.

A Turtle Talk with Crush unit was donated by Walt Disney Imagineering to the Children's Hospital of Orange County in early 2013 to entertain children and their siblings. It is operated twice a day by volunteering Disney cast members.

In May 2016 the theme park attraction added the characters of Dory, Destiny the whale shark, Bailey the beluga whale and Hank the "septopus" (a seven-legged octopus) along with Crush's son Squirt.

Second Night at Animator's Palate on the *Magic, Wonder* and *Fantasy* is a show entitled "Animation Magic" where guests are given a pre-prepared placemat where they can draw the head, body, arms and legs of their own cartoon character. Those placemats are then taken away and at the end of the meal those characters are animated on the screen so that they dance alongside classic Disney characters. The placemats are returned to the guests with a seal declaring the guest a Disney animator.

Enchanted Garden

Disney Design Group artist Ron Cohee did the artwork for the Enchanted Garden menu that features the flowers from Disney's animated feature *Alice in Wonderland* (1951). Cohee was especially excited to illustrate the "bread and butterfly," an obscure character he felt he would never have had the chance to draw anywhere else.

The restaurant was inspired by the elaborate gardens of Versailles in France. During the day, it is reminiscent of a brightly lit cultivated conservatory that feature white trellises with green arches, and custom glass flower-shaped light fixtures up above. More than 600 light panels arch across the ceiling like a glass canopy.

At night, that canopy changes into a nighttime sky filled with stars and the light fixture "flowers" bloom open and are filled with color. Paintings are illuminated differently and the wall sconces open like beautiful folding fans.

Original art depicts lush greenery and at night are illuminated with a nocturnal glow. Ornamental light posts line the formal center promenade. It appears to be ivy climbing the side of the ironworks.

The centerpiece is a seven-foot tall fountain with a cherub Mickey Mouse statue in the center. Mickey is holding a bow and arrow not as a hunter but as a reference to Cupid who is in one of the fountains at Versailles.

Royal Palace

Themed to the classic Disney princesses from the animated films *Cinderella, Snow White and the Seven Dwarfs, Beauty and the Beast* and *Sleeping Beauty*, the elegant setting is reminiscent of the romantic circular ballroom of Prince Charming's castle in *Cinderella* with wall sconces fashioned after those seen in *Beauty and the Beast*. Gold and white faux-marble columns form an inner circle.

Marble floors, luxurious royal carpets, and a hand-blown chandelier in the main dining room made of glass slippers and gold tiaras decorate the room. The location is filled with royal crests, roses and similar elegant touches including chair backs embellished with gilded emblems.

Mosaic tile portraits of princesses including Cinderella, Snow White, Belle and Princess Aurora (Sleeping Beauty) are on the far wall. The portholes are framed with majestic window valances, topped with sparkling tiaras.

Even the bread baskets on the tables are wire re-creations of Cinderella's enchanted coach. The serving staff are attired in appropriate royal uniforms.

The restaurant was meant to appeal to those who love the popular and elaborate Disney Princess franchise.

Cabanas

Cabanas is a buffet-style restaurant open for breakfast, lunch, and dinner (in the evening it transforms into a table service/cooked to order experience) with a wide selection of options in a more casual family atmosphere than the other restaurants.

It is the largest restaurant on the ship in terms of size with both indoor and outdoor seating. It is especially suited for families with children or those who want to sample a little of a number of different items.

The interior area is to suggest "where everyday is a picnic on the beach" including faux palm trees that rise up through the ceiling. The name is a reference to the tent-like structure often found on a beach.

The entrance is a striped canvas foyer so it is like entering a beach cabana. The flock of seagulls from the Disney/Pixar film *Finding Nemo* (2003) is standing up above on the signpost watching as the guests come in. Outside by the elevators is a full three-dimensional figure of Nigel the brown pelican from the film with a fish in his beak.

The two huge seascape mosaic murals also feature characters from the animated feature. These murals were especially created by a team of nine Italian artists working by hand in the time honored tradition. Each mural is more than 25 feet wide and more than 8 feet high and contains approximately 194,500 tiles in 200 colors of hand-crafted Venetian enamel.

Pixar was intimately involved in the designs and the depiction of the individual characters like Nemo, Squirt, Bruce, and more. The team of nine artists created the mosaics based on Pixar designs depicting the underwater world of Australia's Great Barrier Reef and included the characters featured in the motion picture.

There are plaques done up to resemble sand that feature the castles from the Disney theme parks in Hong Kong, Tokyo, Orlando, Anaheim, and Paris, so they are literally "sand castles". Directly across from them are clocks with the actual time in each of those locations.

Meridian Bar

Between the expensive restaurants Palo and Remy located Aft on Deck 12 on the *Disney Dream* and the *Disney Fantasy* is the Meridian Bar.

It is an intimate adults-only area that is open to guests even if they have no reservations at either restaurant though its primary function is to serve as a waiting area for the two restaurants.

From five p.m. to midnight, it serves cocktails or a mixed drink (although beer, wine and coffee are also available), and there is an outside seating for a smoking area, one of the few areas on the ship where smoking is permitted, or to enjoy a quiet sunset.

With windows on three sides, it offers a beautiful panoramic view of the ocean from the back of the ship in a protected environment. Those guests including children not interested in the bar can visit during the afternoon.

There are antique maps on the walls and nautical instruments throughout the room. It also includes compass-point light fixtures as well as an illuminated constellation map above the maitre d' station, since early ships used the stars to guide them to their destination.

In the display cabinet there are multiple authentic nautical books and on the *Disney Dream* there is also a reproduction of the infamous Maltese Falcon statue because "it's the stuff that dreams are made of."

There are passport stamps on the wallpaper, a sextant design on the floor and the rich brown leather couches have luggage straps on them to capture the feel of traveling during the Golden Age of Cruise Ships of the 1930s.

Lights that resemble gas lamps overhang the bar, which is inscribed on the top with the word "Welcome" in many different languages including: Bienvenidos, Willkommen, Benvenuti, Welcome in Mandarin, Velkommen, Hosgeldiniz and Bienvenue.

Palo

Palo restaurants are on all four of the Disney Cruise ships, but the ones on the *Dream* and the *Fantasy* are much more detailed. It was chosen as an homage to the Italian location where the first two DCL cruise ships were built.

The entrance to Palo has a gold-colored Murano blown-glass chandelier that the ship's tour guide described as the "pasta chandelier" since it was reminiscent of spaghetti. The walls of the entrance feature the muted colors of the Italian flag in parallel stripes that lead guests to the interior.

The word "palo" is Italian for "pole" and while the guide insisted that it refers to the poles used by gondoliers in Venice to propel the craft (as does the Disney Cruise Line website), Disney Imagineering friends say that it refers to the colorful poles where gondolas are tied up. The experience of going to a table in the restaurant was meant to bring to mind maneuvering through the twisting canals of Venice to where a gondola would finally "dock."

There is a distinctive pole design on the handmade wine cabinet that had special cradles for the wine bottles.

Along the walls are a series of original paintings depicting Italian locations, and the colors in the paintings were used to match the colors used elsewhere in the restaurant.

On the *Disney Dream*, that floor length painting to the immediate left as guests enter feels rough to the touch because of its beading. That is because it is designed that if a guest took a photo with a flash, it would appear three-dimensional.

Also on the *Disney Dream*, the second painting from the left in the dining room has a hidden Mickey in the clouds.

The interior was designed so all seats, except the ones in the small chef's kitchen, face the windows. That special small dining room was meant to recreate dining with a family in Morono, Italy.

Looking closely, guests will notice that the design of the ceiling mirrors the design on the floor carpet. There are elements of a small family kitchen, including a kitchen hatch so guests can see the meals being prepared.

Remy

Remy restaurant only exists on the *Disney Dream* and the *Disney Fantasy*. Reservations are required. An additional charge is required to dine at Remy which is significantly higher than the additional charge to dine at Palo, in addition to the cost of wine and alcoholic beverages.

It is an adult experience with a strictly enforced dress code requiring suit jackets for men and evening dresses for women.

Remy is the name of the talented culinary French rat from the Disney-Pixar animated feature *Ratatouille* (2007), and he is incorporated into the design in several locations in the restaurant that bears his name.

Entering the dining room, high above on a light fixture is a small statue of Remy in a chef's hat and holding a spoon. The statue was made out of Swarovski crystal and is worth $15,000.

Remy's outline is hidden on the design on the back of the chairs and on the upholstery. His image is also sitting back happily on the lower side of one of the mirrors right across from his older brother Emile on the other side. There are many more "Hidden Remys" to be discovered including the design on the butter plate.

An interesting side note is that the name "Remy" in the film came from the American hairless terrier dog owned by the film's director Brad Bird. Of course, there is still debate whether a rat, usually associated with disease and uncleanliness, is a good image for a restaurant and food despite the success of the film.

Many Disney and Pixar fans may not know that, in 2007, Disney was planning on producing a *Ratatouille* wine with the famous rat on the label to be sold in Costco stores in August of that year.

Disney was going to sell 500 cases to Costco. The wine was sourced from Macon estate Chateau de Messey. Owner Marc Dumont produced it from grapes in his Cruzille vineyard and put the movie label on his regular Bourgogne Chardonnay.

However, Disney cancelled plans when the California Wine Institute put on pressure not to release the wine because the label showed the tiny animated rat holding a tiny glass and its advertising code bans advertising that might appeal to children (by the use of cartoon characters or young models).

Food marketing tie-ins were a challenge because no food company wanted to be associated with a rat, even if it was Disney-Pixar "cute."

In regards to wine, the movie itself features a Chateau Latour and a 1947 Cheval Blanc that the critic Anton Ego drinks. It is considered an excellent vintage (and by some authorities the finest wine in the world and comes from a vineyard in Bordeaux's Saint Emilion) and bottles that are stored properly would remain in a prime drinking window as late as 2050.

At Remy's is a bottle of 1947 Cheval Blanc worth $25,000 (and apparently at least one bottle was sold on the *Disney Fantasy*) on display with supposedly a back-up bottle of it as well. The ship does have a vault and insurance for its most valuable wines.

The film itself includes a wine bottle in the beginning labeled Lasseter Cabernet Sauvignon, a reference to executive producer John Lasseter, a wine bottle labeled Chateau-Bird Champagne named for director Brad Bird and a wine bottle labeled Chateau-Jessup Pauillac Medoc named for production designer Harley Jessup. There are food products in the film named after other Pixar production staff.

As some Disney fans know, Lasseter is deeply involved with wine. Lasseter Family Winery founded in 2000 is in Sonoma County, California. He and his wife Nancy established the eco-friendly winery that produces approximately 1,200 cases of French red wine blends annually although they have the capability of producing more than 6,000 cases.

The wine display case at Remy features bottles from the Lasseter Family Winery and have hand drawn cartoon labels with Pixar characters including Tow Mater; Woody (making a two finger "rabbit ears" sign behind Buzz Lightyear in his space helmet); and Remy, among others, but they are not for sale. Each bottle is autographed by Lasseter and a cast member at the location stated that only Lasseter himself is allowed to uncork these particular bottles.

The staff irons and presses every tablecloth every morning. Those small pedestals next to the tables are where, in the tradition of the Golden Age of Cruising, women would place their purses rather than crudely hanging them on the back of a chair or putting them on the floor.

Over to the left on the table is an authentic silver Christofle vase from the famed French manufacturer. There are only twenty left in the world. One is on the *Disney Dream* and another is on the *Disney Fantasy*.

The china dinnerware was produced by Bernardaud that has been creating the finest porcelain china in France since 1863. Disney had to pay a premium price for the exclusive design rights for the china in Remy at a cost of more than all the other plating combined from all the other restaurants on board.

The private chef's table dining room is called Gusteau's, after famed fictional chef Auguste Gusteau (whose first and last names are anagrams of each other) in the animated feature and who was Remy's cooking idol and inspiration. The room is meant to represent his famous kitchen and is trimmed in gold and gold leaf paint and the lush carpet is handmade.

The painting in this room is a cityscape portrait of Paris as seen through Remy's eyes, but the landmarks depicted like Notre Dame and the Eiffel Tower are not that close together in the real Paris but the guests readily accept that alteration.

Gusteau's restaurant is under the Eiffel Tower. In the room the chairs and drapes are exact reproductions from the film. On the painting depicting Gusteau's kitchen, look to the pots on the right-hand side and you might be able to discern an image of the character of Linguini.

Since only a percentage of wood is allowed on ship because it would be a fire hazard, the ceiling that looks like carved wood is actually plastic, reflecting the Imagineering philosophy that only what can be touched by a guest needs to be real.

The executive chef for Remy is Chef Patrick Albert who was supposedly also one of the inspirations for Chef Gusteau in the movie. In fact, a copy of the handmade carpet in Gusteau's Kitchen dining room was made for Chef Patrick's own home.

In Remy's Wine Vault, which features more than 900 bottles of wine, there is a special ham slicer. The ship's launch was delayed because Chef Patrick told the captain that Jessica had not yet arrived. The captain assumed it was a special guest. It was the name for the ham slicer. The one on the *Disney Fantasy* is named Olga.

There is a sommelier available to assist with wine pairings costing an additional amount above the dining fee. By the way, every bakery good in Vanellope's Sweets and Treats Shop is made on board in the kitchen for Remy. Both Palo and Remy use all Frette dining linens.

Founded in 1860 in France, and now based in Milan, Italy (so it ties in with both the Italian Palo and French Remy), Frette created custom-design plush bath towels and deluxe bed linens for the *Disney Fantasy* and the *Disney Dream* with what is regarded as the world's finest cotton from El Amria in Egypt.

Disney Dream District Nightclubs

The District is a nighttime adult entertainment area located aft on deck 4 on the *Disney Dream*. It is designed to be a sophisticated location at night, a sort of adult playground. There are five interconnected venues (Pink, Skyline, Evolution, 687, and District Lounge) but each has its own individual identity.

In the hallways are life-sized black silhouettes of the paparazzi and others who are being held back behind a red rope and stanchions and not allowed to the "in" spots where the cruise line guests are. Originally, the paparazzi cameras would flash randomly but that was disabled because guests thought that their photos were actually being taken (like on a Disney theme park attraction) and would stand there and pose and later complained when they couldn't find the photos at Shutters.

The pixie dust design on the carpet leads guests to the restrooms and the other lounges.

At 10:45 p.m. a nice buffet is set out for roughly an hour between the District bar and the restrooms to not only alleviate a case of late night munchies but also to help absorb some of that alcohol that is being consumed.

It is a reasonably upscale buffet that includes different offerings each night including tiny sandwiches, veggies, Bruschetta bread, mini-pizzas, and bite-size desserts, so it is much more appealing that leaving to go to the upper deck quick serve locations for more mundane snacks. It is only available for about an hour. At roughly the same time, Cove Café has a free antipasto platter available.

Pink

Pink is a cocktail lounge designed to seem as if guests were immersed inside a bottle of effervescent pink champagne.

This intimate location is characterized by flowing, curvilinear shapes with back-lit glass "bubbles" inset into the wall that go from tiny on the floor to larger near the ceiling just like champagne bubbles bubbling up.

A pink elephant reminiscent of one from the Disney animated feature *Dumbo* (1940) appears in random locations to dance in the bubbles. In the film, Dumbo and his mouse companion Timothy inadvertently drink from a water bucket spiked with alcohol and dream of fantastical pink elephants "on parade" in their nightmare, an allusion to the belief that people who are drunk hallucinate unusual things like pink elephants.

Of course, Dumbo himself is not used as an image, just a tiny pink representative done in the same Disney art style of the movie, because, for one reason, Dumbo is associated with the *Dream*'s sister ship, the *Disney Fantasy*, which has its own champagne bar, the French-themed Ooh La La that has no pink elephants but is decorated more like a French boudoir.

That image of a happy, smiling pink elephant is looking upward and standing on one leg pops up randomly in the different bubbles for a very few seconds.

Some chairs in the lounge even resemble elephant ears, surrounding a guest for a private conversation.

Lighting creates the effect of cascading champagne. Behind the bar there is a lighting fixture that represents the bubbles rushing to the mouth of the bottle and exploding after the cork pops. Sculpted-glass chandelier light fixtures look like upside down champagne flutes awaiting a chance to capture that champagne. The detailing along the front of the bar is meant to resemble the wire cage surrounding a champagne bottle cork.

Taittinger has created two champagnes exclusively for sale aboard the *Disney Dream*: a Brut featuring the *Disney Dream* ship on the label, dedicated to the *Dream*'s inaugural year, and Prestige Rosé Champagne, the label of which is decorated with Pink's mascot pink elephant.

Each bottle costs about $700, although it can be bought by the glass (in a specially designed glass that is hand washed and taken care of so that the glass does not taint the flavor of the product) for roughly $20.

There is a fairly inexpensive wine tasting held at Pink during the afternoon led by the head sommelier on the *Dream* where, for roughly $25, guests can sample four different champagnes that are full glasses, not little tasting pours. However, seating is limited to just ten guests so reservations should be made early at the Guest Services desk.

687

"687" is the name of the pub and sports bar lounge with multiple LCD televisions on the *Disney Dream*.

What is the significance of using that particular number as the name of this bar?

It is bad luck to call a vessel by its official name before its launch, so during construction it is referred to by its "block number," the vessel number marked on every piece of steel and item used to build the ship.

This number refers to the fact that the *Disney Dream* was the 687th built by the Meyer Werft shipyard in Papenburg, Germany.

The keel (the central beam of the ship) laying ceremony is the first time the ship begins to really take shape after many years of design work and planning. The ceremony is when the first block—or section— of the ship is lowered into the building dock and a coin is placed under the keel for good fortune. Sometimes the coin is welded to the keel.

That first block for the *Disney Dream* weighed roughly 380 tons and it would take 80 blocks total for the entire ship.

Doing the honors of placing the coin was Captain Tom Forberg assisted by a costumed Donald Duck, the mascot of the *Disney Dream*, on August 26, 2009.

Disney Cruise Line states: "Placing a coin on the keel of the ship at the beginning of its build is an age-old tradition that solicits good fortune for the vessel during construction and throughout its seagoing."

According to old sea tales, if the ship was damaged, the keel coin could be retrieved to pay for repairs or assistance. If the ship sunk, then the coin would guarantee that the spirit of the ship would live on while the wood rotted away on the ocean bottom. Yet another version for the practice was that sailors who died at sea would have payment for Charon to ferry them across the River Styx into the underworld.

Originally, the idea of a keel coin came from the practice of placing a coin under the mast of a sailing ship for luck that has been documented back to the time of the Roman Empire but was in practice perhaps even earlier, according to some sources, who have located the wrecks of even more ancient sailing vessels.

When Walt Disney was told about this long time tradition by Admiral Joe Fowler, Walt personally put a silver dollar under each of the three masts of the sailing ship *Columbia* at Disneyland before its first sailing.

On the right wall near the entrance to the "687" pub is a frame with photos of the placement of the keel coin as well as a replica of it. A limited number of bronze replicas of the coin were available for sale to guests during the maiden voyage.

"687" is open during the day, often for various presentations, so it is possible to take the entire family, no matter the age, into the location and see the frame with the coin before the pub becomes an adult-only hangout in the evening.

Skyline

The concept for this dark lounge is that it is located in a penthouse apartment overlooking the city. There are seven windows (actually 65-inch high definition screens) behind the bar that give an overhead panoramic view of five different cities that rotate every 15 minutes when Tinker Bell drops pixie dust on them.

Those cities are New York, Chicago, Rio de Janeiro, Paris and Hong Kong, and they are not still pictures, but a living environment with moving traffic, blinking neon signs and lights in the apartment building going on and off to indicate the coming and going of the residents. Mickey Mouse waves to sharp-eyed and patient guests from inside a tiny apartment in Paris.

These "windows to the world" as Imagineers dubbed them transform from day to night, so if someone stays there long enough they can catch the sunset and evening turn to late at night. The lounge even serves signature cocktails inspired by the featured cities.

Not only does the soft background music reflect each city (eg. Chicago has jazz, New York has Broadway show tunes, etc.) but the travel poster on the wall opposite the bar is an Enchanted Art screen and shift as well to reflect the particular city.

Because the lounge is small and decorated in darker colors, the menus are designed to "light up" so guests can see the selections clearly. Looking at just the right angle (from over on the right hand side), the coals in the "digital" fireplace form a silhouette of Cinderella Castle at the Walt Disney World Resort's Magic Kingdom.

Evolution

The bar is, according to Disney publicity, "an artistic interpretation of the transformation of a butterfly....emerging from a chrysalis." The bar is in the shape of a chrysalis and on the dance floor, the ceiling is in the shape of the wings of a multi-colored butterfly.

Supposedly, a visitor goes through a similar transformation as they move from the entrance which is dark and narrow like a birth canal to the bar to the dance floor that bursts open in color.

A lot of yellow, orange and red lights arranged in the shape of butterfly wings are hung around the club. The swirling trails of light on the ceiling are meant to represent butterflies in flight.

In the evenings, Evolution also hosts some live entertainment, including magicians, comedians, live singers, and karaoke. During the day, a variety of presentations are held in the location because it is such a large venue.

O'Gills, the Lucky Fish

On the *Disney Magic* and *Disney Fantasy*, the sports bar is called O'Gill's Pub. It is about as Irish as a McDonald's Shamrock Shake or a box of Lucky Charms cereal.

The guide on the ship claimed that "O'Gill's Pub is based on the Disney film *Darby O'Gill and the Little People* (1959). If you remember the film, it featured leprechauns and one fell in a river and was rescued by a fish. The leprechaun granted him a wish and the fish just wanted a place where he could share a pint with his new friend and that is the story of O'Gill's."

There is no such episode in the film, or in Darby's fanciful stories, where a leprechaun was rescued by fish, let alone given a public house for drinking.

O'Gill's features a cartoonish painting of a pipe-smoking leprechaun standing on a bank near his pot of gold clinking glasses with a sleepy-eyed, smiling pink fish in a black derby and tie standing upright on its tail in the nearby body of water.

Of course, the name of the pub also references that a fish would have gills and the expression "drunk to the gills" fit in as well. Drunk to the gills was an expression that meant you were so full of alcohol that you were swimming in it "up to your gills."

When the *Disney Magic* cruise ship launched in 1998, this bar was called Off Beat. In 2003, it was re-themed and renamed

Diversions. Today, it is called O'Gills after the one that originated on the *Disney Fantasy*.

According to the official Disney Cruise website:

> O'Gill's Pub is a spirited Irish bar located on Deck 4, Aft in the Europa district on the *Disney Fantasy*. From the whimsical to the cosmopolitan, each venue in Europa is distinctly inspired by the very best in European travel.
>
> Dark woods and brass accents are reminiscent of the friendly neighborhood pubs throughout Ireland—and flat-screen televisions give O'Gill's Pub a welcome modern-day twist. Exclusively for Guests ages 18 and older, O'Gill's Pub is a great spot for adults to unwind after a fun-filled day, catch the big game and kick off a night exploring the entertainment of Europa.

O'Gill's offers a red lager draft made especially for the pub, as well as its own private label Irish Cream and vintage Irish whisky.

Apparently, its popularity on the *Disney Fantasy* prompted its inclusion on the *Disney Magic* for its After Hours adult club area. O'Gills does not theme in as well with the other two *Disney Magic* nightclub venues: Keys (an Art Deco piano bar meant to suggest the Golden Age of Hollywood and similar locations on Sunset Boulevard) and Fathoms (a generic ocean themed dance club space with overhead jellyfish lighting fixtures that light up—thanks to 400 strands of fiber optics and 250 different colors created by Impact Lighting of Orlando, Florida).

Here is the original story about O'Gills in verse that I found that had been written by Imagineering:

The Legend of O'Gills

> This is the legend of O'Gills the lucky fish, who saved the Leprechaun and was granted a wish.
>
> You see, the Leprechaun was kind of a slacker, and carrying his pot o' gold made him quite knackered.
>
> He stopped for a drink from the loch, when a crab pulled him underwater in a shock.
>
> The Leprechaun was about to drown, but luckily our hero, O'Gills, was around.
>
> With a puff of his pipe, O'Gills tipped his hat, and used his tail to give that crab a deadly whack.
>
> The Leprechaun swam away and thankful he was, and then offered a wish to O'Gills without pause.

The Leprechaun expected a wish for riches or a yoke; he says wishes are never quare, and usually a joke.

But O'Gills puffed his pipe and remained nonchalant, because he knew exactly the kind of wish he wants.

O'Gills smiled and said "gargle" to the Little Man, and then asked him if he could give him a hand.

You see, O'Gills didn't need stuff or riches to spend; he just wanted to share a pint with his new little friend.

So let's raise our glasses for O'Gills wish, and drink to new friends and a lucky fish.

Somewhat frustrating is that the official Disney Cruise Line website lists both "O'Gill's Pub" *and* "O'Gills Pub" as the name of the location, switching back and forth several times on the same page from using a apostrophe.

There is also an official song for O'Gill's Pub, and here it is. I suppose the intention was that if the group that night was inebriated enough that the bartenders might lead everyone in the pub in a rousing rendition of this song although I have never seen that happen.

The Ballad of O'Gills

O'Gills, O'Gills the lucky fish, O'Gills, O'Gills Please make a wish.

Let's tip our hats and have a chat, With O'Gills the lucky fish!

O'Gills, O'Gills The fighting fish, O'Gills, O'Gills You are Irish

Let's join the group And have some scoops With O'Gills the lucky Fish!

O'Gills, O'Gills The drinking fish O'Gills, O'Gills Please make a wish

Let's share a glass With a fine Irish lass And O'Gills the lucky fish!

O'Gills, O'Gills the lucky fish, O'Gills, O'Gills Please make a wish.

Let's tip our hats and have a chat, With O'Gills the lucky fish!

O'Gills, O'Gills The fighting fish, O'Gills, O'Gills You are Irish

Let's join the group And have some scoops With O'Gills the lucky Fish!

O'Gills, O'Gills The drinking fish O'Gills, O'Gills Please make a wish

Let's share a glass With a fine Irish lass And O'Gills the lucky fish!

Vanellope's Sweets and Treats

Wreck-It Ralph was a 2012 animated feature film from Walt Disney Pictures that recounts the story of an arcade game villain named Ralph wandering through several other video games in an attempt to become a hero. One of those games is Sugar Rush, a racing game in a land made entirely of candy and featuring a go-kart racer named Vanellope von Schweetz.

This new candy shop, unique to just the *Disney Dream*, so far, recreates that experience. Purchasing any sweet treats here is an additional charge, like at any of the other shipboard shops.

During the *Disney Dream*'s three week 2015 dry dock, Vanellope's Sweets and Treats was added, replacing the former Arr-cade (a dark game room with arcade games) on the starboard side, Aft area near Cabanas on Deck 11. Disney claims that arcade game rooms are no longer the attraction they once were, before kids started playing the games on their own mobile devices.

There is an entrance inside Cabanas, as well as on the pool deck just outside the door to Cabanas.

When you first enter the space from the outside deck, there is a mural of the Starting Line from the racing game, a sculpture of Vanellope's racing go-kart, and a sculpture of King Candy waving the checkered flag from the winner's tri-level podium. The racetrack circles the entire interior space as can be seen by the design on the floor.

The grandstands on top of the candy dispenser are exact replicas from the ones in the film. Each grandstand represents a racer in the game. The background music in the shop is a combination of music from the film, 8-bit video game music, and J-pop, to match with the theme of the shop.

Behind the sculpture of Vanellope hanging upside down is a mural of the Candy Cane Forest where she first met Wreck-It Ralph. Her go-kart is in front of a racetrack background and was specifically made as a photo opportunity.

The festive shop offers 20 flavors of gelato and 16 flavors of ice cream, all handcrafted and often different each day. There are more than 28 different toppings that can be added, as well. The whipped cream is made fresh every day.

The six artisan sundaes on the menu include two signature ones served in special souvenir cups. Families can indulge in the

Ralph's Family Challenge Sundae, eight scoops of ice cream and eight toppings in a 52-ounce winner's trophy cup.

A solo ice cream lover might try Vanellope's Go-Kart Sundae, three scoops and five toppings in a souvenir plastic go-kart shaped dish that features wheels that move.

The shop's animated leader board, designed to look like the one in the movie, showcases the day's trending sundaes. All six start the day on the board, and as they're purchased, the leading sundaes move up the board to highlight the guest favorites that day.

Eclairs, designer cookies, cupcakes, candy apples, rice krispy treats, macaroons, truffles, tarts, and specialty brownies on a stick are just some of the delicious treats offered, along with bulk candy from dispensers. A colorful candy assortment, some of it with Ralph's image, is available, along with signature lollipops atop King Candy's lollipop tree.

Every now and then, the bald green head of Sour Bill (the majordomo of King Candy's sour ball henchmen) snores and then emerges from beneath a pile of gumballs in a large glass globe on top of the red gasoline pump in the middle to lament in a sad, monotonous voice: "Hey, do you see your favorite racer on the leader board? I'm so happy for you."

He then continues periodically to say something else equally sour like: "They named the dessert after the racers although I don't know why Vaneloppe gets her own sundae.", "Don't put me in your mouth. Please don't put me in your filthy mouth again, Ralph", "Everyone's going to Taffyta's after the big race. I wasn't invited", "Despite what everyone thinks, I am not a cough drop. Please wash your hands. Thank you", "Glitch! No. False Alarm. Please go back to enjoying the race", "There's lots of different candies here and we are all happy to meet you", "Of course I'm not happy. They don't call me Sour Bill for nothing", "Even the glitches get more respect around here than me."

Rich Moore, who directed the film and was the voice of Sour Bill, recorded new lines just for this experience. There are thirty different sayings.

This surprise is just one of many in this new immersive environment. WDI Creative Designer Danny Handke felt it was a challenge to bring the story of the film into such a limited space. The design process began around 2013 and construction happened 24/7 when the ship was in dry dock.

In case you don't remember, the names of the other racers in the film are Taffyta Muttonfudge, Crumbelina Di Caramello, Gloyd Orangeboar, Adorabeezle Winterpop, Citrusella Flugpucker, Torvald Batterbutter, Nougetsia Brumblestain, Sticky Wipplesnit, Minty Zaki (a tribute to Japanese animator and director Hayao Miyazaki, one of John Lasseter's idols), Snowanna Rainbeau, Rancis Fluggerbutter, Jubileena Bing-Bing, Swizzle Malarkey, and Candlehead.

Castaway Cay

From the sign posted at the Pelican Point tram stop on the island and in the hardcover stateroom book:

> Three explorers set sail to the scattered out islands of the Bahamas in search of fame and fortune. They brought along their families and a diverse crew. Through mild mishap and extreme good fortune, they located the objects of their desire, sunken treasures and the secret of youth.
>
> Though cast away on this island, they had no desire to leave due to the breathtaking beauty of this tropical paradise. Visitors to this island can still see the original structures built by the explorers and take part in many of the same pleasures our castaways enjoyed years ago.
>
> Disney Cruise Line welcomes you to the island paradise of your dreams, Castaway Cay.

Castaway Cay: The Real Story

Castaway Cay (pronounced "key") opened officially for the first time on July 30, 1998. Cay refers to a small, low-elevation, sandy island on the surface of a coral reef and comes from the Spanish word "cayo." Key West was originally called "Cayo Hueso".

The Disney Company leased Gorda (meaning "fat" in Spanish) Cay that is part of a string of islands named the Abacos from the Bahamian government in 1996 for a hundred years. The lease is set to expire in 2096.

It took eighteen months, more than twenty-five million dollars and 50,000 truckloads of sand to create an appealing "castaway community" on this exclusive port of call for Disney Cruise Line ships.

"The stage was set by Mother Nature," said senior development manager Jim Durham. "We just provided the backdrop."

The closest island is roughly eight miles away. Disney had to blast and dredge a thirty-five foot deep berth for the original two ships with that material used to create the berth pier.

To accommodate the two larger ships (*Disney Dream* and *Disney Fantasy*), which were introduced beginning in 2011, the island underwent several enhancements, including lengthening the dock, expanding the family beach, adding food and beverage areas as well as other amenities.

The buildings purposely look as if they had been patched together after a shipwreck and are weathered from having been there for decades before Disney found them, much like some of the architecture at the Typhoon Lagoon water park at the Walt Disney World Resort that opened in 1989.

Art Director Ken Danberry said:

> The overall look of the buildings was critical to the storyline. We relied heavily on color and theming to create, not a resort, but a mature tropical island with touches of present day.

Bob Holderbaum who was the show production designer added that the buildings were painted with bright colors typical of the tropics and then antiquing techniques were used to create the natural weathered look. More than three thousand individual props were installed from airplanes to fishing poles.

The entire infrastructure had to be created including originally twenty-nine buildings strong enough to withstand up to 120 mph winds.

The Disney Company planted a variety of flora, including the gumbo limbo (Bursera simaruba) that natives call "the tourist tree" because of its red, peeling bark resembling a sunburned tourist. Imagineers had to design it so that the landscaping looked natural and not a simulated environment. The task was complicated by the fact that the Cay is an arid island with limited rainfall.

Over 800 mature coconut palms were planted along with other drought and salt tolerant plants such as scaevola and sea grapes.

Working with a contractor who was experienced in building local marinas, docks and piers, Disney had to literally ship in every truck, bulldozer and more to the location. The majority of the construction crew were local Bahamians, most of whom were trained specifically to complete the project.

The island is a prime example of the Disney Company's commitment to the environment, including restoring the health of coral reefs by transplanting long-spined sea urchins and fostering their growth; protecting and monitoring endangered loggerhead sea turtle nests; and using solar panels in backstage areas to fuel water heaters for bathing, dishwashing and laundry for Disney Cruise Line personnel living on the island.

Sea water is desalinated for drinking with two reverse osmosis water processors. Some water is procured in Port Canaveral and delivered to Castaway Cay by the ships to an 80,000 gallon fresh water storage tank on the island. Backstage is a sewage treatment plant.

An innovative recycling program re-purposes used cooking oil from the ships' galleys and combines it with diesel fuel to power machinery on the island. The program reduces waste and carbon dioxide emissions, saving up to 8,000 gallons of traditional fuel each year.

Roughly a hundred and fifty cast members are inhabitants of the island (with contracts running from four to nine months) and when a ship docks, the crew on the ship supplement the staff on the island, especially in handling the food and retail areas.

The island encompasses 1,100 acres of land (only about 55 acres are currently being used). It is 3.1 miles long and 2.2 miles wide. It is 225 nautical miles from Port Canaveral, Florida.

Gorda Cay was located just to the north of an active trade route in the 1700s and rumors of pirates perhaps visiting the location were common.

The island offers many hidden alcoves and was believed to provide great hiding spots for pirates to anchor and lie in wait to ambush passing ships. Two treasure hunters from Nassau in the 1950s came across a few objects just off the shoals of the island including three coins and a 72 pound silver ingot. Markings showed the objects belonged to Spain's King Philip IV, and that the treasures were aboard the *San Pedro*, a Spanish Galleon that sank in 1733.

The island was relatively rock free and fertile, and eventually a tiny village appeared on the southern shore as a safe haven for fishermen in rough seas.

In the 1960s, businessman Alvin Tucker bought 150 acres and put in a small airstrip to accommodate his visits. Unfortunately, that airstrip became an appealing location for smugglers and drug runners who took it over and eventually bought the land from Tucker, who no longer felt safe.

Within the next two decades, it was notorious for being an armed compound with big, vicious dogs dissuading visitors. A huge cocaine bust worth more than one hundred million dollars in 1983 was the beginning of the end for criminal activity on the island with the drug lord and his cronies being sent off to prison.

In fact, the island became more "friendly" and the beach in the Touchstone film *Splash* (1984) where Madison the mermaid (Daryl Hannah) rescues Allen (Tom Hanks) when he falls into the waters of Cape Cod was not filmed in New England but at the Serenity Bay area when the island was known as Gorda Cay.

The Original Imagineering Back Story

The Disney Imagineers created a convoluted storyline for Castaway Cay in much the same spirit as the overly complicated storyline for the original Pleasure Island to explain why things were there and where names for buildings originated. Some of those elements still exist today, including the name of the post mistress of the island.

In the early 1920s, three explorers and their families set sail to the scattered islands of the Bahamas in search of fame and fortune. Shortly into their adventure, they encountered the winds of a wild ocean storm that landed their ship upon the island now called Castaway Cay.

While at first the troupe was fearful of impending demise, they soon became intoxicated by the tropical beauty of the island.

The leader of the expedition was a professor of paleontology from Chicago by the name of Cecil Chamberlain. "Wormy," as he was called by his friends, was in search of the skeletal remains of a prehistoric sperm whale, the Physeter catodon, which, by good fortune, he eventually discovered on the island. With his search at an end, he decided to retire on Castaway Cay, devoting the remainder of his years to the excavation of the whale.

Professor Chamberlain had hired Captain Sandy Morton, his wife and his sons to lead the crew on their adventure. Captain Morton, having lived his whole life at sea, promised his wife that, after the storm, he would leave the life at sea to live on land. So the captain spent his days carving signs for the simple streets and rustic buildings that were sprouting up as the castaways made the island their home.

Chamberlain's young protege at the University of Chicago, Dr. Max Profitt, had also joined the expedition, but not in search of whales. Profitt joined to look for sunken treasure. The discovery of a 300-year-old Spanish galleon, laden with gold and jewels, at the bottom of the lagoon was everything he had hoped to find.

However, instead of snatching his treasure and returning home, he decided to stay on the island and set up dive trails in order to share these amazing artifacts with others. Gil, the captain's oldest son, and his three brothers opened Gil's Fins and Boats to take charge of the dive trails and all other water activities, such as snorkeling and boating.

A third explorer, E'Lan Vital, or "Doc," had signed on board in the hopes of discovering the Fountain of Youth, which he thought was on one of the hundreds of Caribbean islands. Though he never found the fountain, he did observe the youthful energy of the island. Content with his findings, Doc decided to open the first island clinic.

Doc's wife, Mere Vital, was a well-preserved beauty who decided that the island (paradise though it was) lacked one of her greatest pleasures—shopping. Determined to offer this added activity to the island's option, and armed with years of experience inspecting goods up and down the Eastern seaboard, Mere commandeered a small island hut that had once been used to store supplies.

Her first foray into the mercantile trade was an offering of seashells, gathered from the nearby beach, and painted in rich colors. She fashioned them into jewelry, designed from her wonderful memories of shopping in New York City.

Early into Mere's shell enterprise, cleverly called She Sells Seashells, Chamberlain stepped in as a voice of conscience. His years of scientific study and passion for fossils and artifacts led him to believe that taking shells from the seashore disturbed the natural ecological balance of the island and robbed countless sea creatures of their homes.

He therefore persuaded her to pursue another product for her shop. She, determined to succeed, reluctantly crossed out the word "Seashells" on the sign she had hung across the front of her shop and set out to create products that reflected the essential quality of the island paradise.

Shortly after the castaways had landed on the island, they befriended a local man named Grinz Alott. Grinz showed these city folk the way of the island, from following local customs like the great Junkanoo celebrations of the Bahamas. It was the essence of this festival that Mere decided to capture in the costumes and clothing sold at her boutique. The change proved profitable not only for Mere but also for the ecological well-being of the island.

Another enterprising woman among the castaways was Marian Profitt, the young wife of Dr. Profitt. Early on, she saw the need to educate the children of the island, as the castaways brought nearly a dozen with them.

She set up Discovery Tents in a sandy cove near the whale dig, a convenient place for the children to study science, nature, music, literature, and the culture of this beautiful region. Together she and Chamberlain taught the children conservation awareness so that they would understand the importance of preserving the natural habitat of the island's flora and fauna.

One of her brighter students was her own daughter, Molly, who explored every inch of this tropical wonderland. In fact, it was Molly and her best friend, Seth, who first ventured beyond the wild side of the island to look for the nesting place of the chick carnie. Every day Molly and Seth searched for the bird from sunrise to sunset, stopping only when they heard the dinner bell calling Seth to work.

Seth's father, Cookie, and his family had been the cooks on the ship and later ran Cookie's BBQ, still the only place to get good Southern cooking on the island.

The morning after the castaways landed on the island, Doc was deep in the forest looking for his fountain of youth but found instead a man asleep in the cockpit of a downed plane. Cameron ("Cam") O'Flage was an expatriate from Australia and an island hopper in the Bahamas. He had run out of gas during the storm but landed safely in the marsh on the island.

The castaways gave him some of their supplies, and Cookie shipped up Cam's first real meal in weeks. Wanting to give something back, Cam opened and outfitted the bar down at the end of the runway, using parts from his downed plane. Out of respect and gratitude for the hospitality of his new friends, he names it the Castaway Air Bar.

When supplies were getting low and word was getting out about the island paradise the castaways built, they contracted with locals to build a "real" runway as opposed to the one carved by Cam's plane the night he arrived. This and the boat dock were the castaways' connection to the outside world.

When air traffic was no longer needed, they marked an "X" on the runway and grounded the two Beechcraft planes, one on each end. From that point on, they relied solely on the sea for outside contact, including mail.

The Castaway Cay Post Office was opened by May B. Tamara, the first postmistress of Castaway Cay, who fell in love with and eventually married one of Captain Morton's sons. The wedding was a lively celebration; people came from miles around to be part of the festivities.

Cookie cooked an authentic Southern meal, Grinz told stories. Mere designed May's dress. Cam served the champagne. Molly and Seth were the flower girl and ring bearer, respectively. And Captain Morton presided over the ceremony.

Even when the DCL debuted, it would be rare to find even one person who knew this complete story or even knew that it existed. It was too complicated for guests to remember all those names and connections.

For most guests, Castaway Cay was simply a desert island inhabited by castaways and that was all they needed to know. In fact, if a guest goes on an additional cruise, they become a member of the Castaway Club with some additional benefits, including a special lanyard, that increase with each cruise.

The Revised Back Story

Nobody including the staff of the DCL remembered the original, too elaborate back story of Castaway Cay and so it soon faded. A more concise version of the story was created when new additions were made to the island in 2010 that incorporated some of the elements from the original and was included in the hardcover book in each cabin entitled *A Complete Guide to Your Disney Cruise*.

The little dot of land in the vast Caribbean Sea had different meanings to different people. For explorers, there had long been tales of the island's magical properties that seemed to "stop time" for anyone that was lucky enough to find the island and come ashore.

The indigenous people of the Caribbean long believed the island had mystical powers that would wash away all the worries of life. They would often stop there to absorb the island's power before traveling on to other bits of land scattered throughout the vast ocean.

The crews of sailing ships, lost at sea, told stories of discovering a small speck of land that suddenly appeared out of nowhere and allowed them to nurse their ships as well as themselves back to good health. Castaway Cay was no ordinary island. It was a great mystery.

For as long as anyone could remember, there was another legend about Castaway Cay, a belief that eventually brought about the discovery of the island's true secrets. See, the tropical island, with the calmest water in the Caribbean and some of the most tranquil beaches ever to be seen was also known as a hiding place for treasure...pirate treasure.

Castaway Cay made perfect sense as a hiding place for pirate treasure. The coastal waters, calm almost all year round, made sailing in with captured booty a very easy task for even the most rum-soaked pirate crew. It was the ideal hiding place, and word soon spread that Castaway Cay was literally the treasure of the Caribbean, that is, if you could find it.

So in the 1930s, a group of treasure hunters gathered all of the information they could, from hand-drawn maps to the diaries of long-passed sailors, and set out to find Castaway Cay. They packed a cargo boat with supplies and modern equipment and set sail from the East Coast of the United States. They told no one where they were headed, not even friends or family.

As they set sail that spring evening, this group of men, women, and even some children had no idea that their lives were about to change and that their journey would end with them never leaving the island that they so desperately sought.

After traveling down the coast for three days, the treasure-hunting ship turned and sailed at top speed into the waters of the Caribbean. They charted a course that led the ship straight to the eastern shores of Castaway Cay. As the captain and crew dropped anchor, the group of treasure hunters all stood on deck and marveled at the beautiful little island.

With the cargo ship anchored near the lagoon, the treasure hunters quickly unloaded their gear and started to search the island. "Where would pirates hide that treasure?" they wondered as they looked in the forest, moved aside rocks, and dug on the beaches.

A full week passed and not one bit of treasure could be found, leading to confusion and many arguments among the group of seekers. They soon realized that their easy fortune was really a fool's errand. There was simply no treasure on Castaway Cay. They made a plan to pack up and leave the next morning. But then, the mysterious storm arrived.

The sky turned very dark and an unusually thick fog rolled in. Large waves started to crash against the shore. As they sat in their tents, dry from the rain, some thought they could hear their ship groan as it was pushed against the coral.

When they all walked down to the beach the next morning, one thing was obvious: their ship was gone. They were now stuck on Castaway Cay.

Like most new castaways, the group built signal fires, wrote messages with rocks on the beach for the rare chance an airplane would fly over, and even put messages in bottles. They also surveyed their supplies and realized that they were very lucky to bring so much food and so many tools ashore.

Between the easy-to-catch fish, as well as their own canned goods and bottled drinks, they would have plenty of food and water to last for a long time. As they searched around the island

and on the beaches, the castaways would occasionally find bits of manmade hardware from ship wrecks and spilled cargo that would add to their supplies.

After the initial fear of being stranded passed, this industrious crew of seamen and treasure hunters soon built up a village. They created little places to eat, small cabana-sized huts to relax, and even tiny shops to sell each other bits of merchandise and things that they made. With a number of children amongst them, fun was a top priority.

Everyone worked together to build a series of beach and recreation centers. They called the water slide Pelican Plunge and a fun water play area they named Spring-A-Leak. When some of the castaways found whale bones, they named the site Monstro Point, after the sea monster in a famous storybook. The more the former treasure hunters build up their little village, the happier they became. They figured if they were going to be stuck on an island, this was a great island to be stuck on.

Then one day a plane flew overhead. The small cargo plane, flying food and drinks to another Caribbean island, started to lose power over Castaway Cay. The pilot finally crash landed into the jungle near the island's northeastern coast. As he climbed out of his wrecked plane thinking he was in the middle of nowhere, imagine his surprise when he was met by a group of castaways who welcomed him and offered him a tasty meal.

When he asked where such a meal was possibly prepared on a deserted island, they answered, "Cookie's BBQ of course". The pilot toured the island and realized he had never been to such an amazing place. The island had beautiful weather, calm water, and the friendliest people he'd met in all his many flights abroad.

The village had everything one needed to relax. With his plane damaged and radio out of range, the newest castaway decided to do all that he could to help contribute to the island paradise. Using the drinks on his plane as a start, he built the Castaway Air Bar right near the quietest beach on the island, a place they soon called Serenity Beach. He also led the building of the island's first airstrip, not as a way to leave one day, but as a signal to other planes to stop by and visit, something that eventually occurred.

As time went by, the original treasure-hunting castaways had many opportunities to leave the island as a number of planes and ships discovered them, yet every time they were given the chance, the group unanimously decided to stay. Many of the would-be rescuers also decided to stay.

As more people joined the original group of castaways, the island became better supplied. New activities and destinations were added to the original village, including places to snorkel, ride bikes, and buy exotic trinkets and treats. But the spirit of the island always remained the same.

Castaway Cay was, and still is, a place to visit, relax, and let the troubles of the outside world disappear. It is a place that several generations of castaways have enjoyed and still call their home. It is a place that doesn't hide treasure, but is the treasure itself.

While this story included some of the new additions to Castaway Cay and tried to simplify the tale and the many characters, it still proved too daunting and unnecessary for both guests and cast members so a final revision was shortened to only two paragraphs.

Among other locations, it is on signage by the Pelican Point tram stop and in the hardcover book in the stateroom cabins and is now considered the official story of the island.

The Real "Castaways"

Roughly one hundred and fifty people live on Castaway Cay. The numbers fluctuate during the busy and "off" seasons. These real "castaways" are employees who interact with the guests from the ships, island maintenance, horticulturalists, boat captains, landscapers, engineers, marine specialists, lifeguards and more.

There are also a small number of cast members that commute by boat from a neighboring island.

Some of the DCL ship's cast members temporarily occupy the island as well when the ship docks to work at the food and beverage locations, custodial, retail and entertainment (the costumed characters). Food and other supplies are brought in by the DCL ships and are off loaded when they dock.

All of the resident inhabitants live in the Crew Compound. They have a crew beach, gym, football pitch, indoor recreation area, crew mess and, of course, they live on a beautiful, secluded Caribbean island. When a ship is docked, if the cast member has some time off, they can go on the ship to relax, watch movies in the theater and more.

When their contract is up or they have some time off, the island employees can board one of the cruise ships as they are leaving the island and get a ride back to Cape Canaveral. Disney Cruise Line keeps several staterooms unoccupied to be sure there is room for them.

For roughly two decades, the island manager has been Guenter Schmid who has been there since the beginning of construction on the island. He is happy living on the island that he describes as "a subtropical paradise".

The landscapers start their day with a meeting at seven o'clock in the morning. Not only do they have to maintain the green look but keep the foliage under control so that among other things coconuts don't fall on a guests' heads since there are thousands of coconut trees. There has never been a reported incident of that happening.

SEAcrets of Castaway Cay

The Plane. The emblem on the plane at the end of the runaway with Donald Duck wearing aviator goggles and riding on a yellow lightning bolt is an homage to the insignia designed by the Disney Studios for the 438th Fighter Squadron during World War II. It is similar but with a few variations so it doesn't specifically duplicate the original.

Flying Dutchman. When filming in the Caribbean finished in spring 2006 on the *Pirates of the Caribbean* movies *Dead Man's Chest* and *At the World's End*, the 175 foot full-sized replica of Davy Jones' infamous ship *The Flying Dutchman* was put on display starting July 2006 at Castaway Cay Lagoon near Marge's Barges next to the main docking area, moored in a quiet cove to help promote the films and offer a unique scenic photo backdrop opportunity for guests.

As of November 2010, the ship was removed and taken to another location on the island, where it was dismantled over several weeks since weather, time and the elements had taken their toll on the movie prop.

The Giant Palm Tree. One of the unusual features on the island is a giant palm tree that towers over the surrounding foliage. It is actually a not-so-cleverly disguised communications tower located in the middle of the island disguised as a palm tree in order to keep with the theming of a castaway island. The communications tower is used for the local Bahamas cell phone carrier, as well as to transmit radio frequencies for cast members who work and live on the island.

Where's The Tender? Most ships use tender boats to ferry guests to and from their islands, but Disney built its own pier to accommodate even the largest of its ships and built a breaker wall so it is a safe harbor. This allows guests even in inclement weather easy access to the island by simply walking off the ship.

Stingrays. DCL partnered with the marine staff of Epcot's The Seas with Nemo and Friends to create the twenty to thirty minute hands-on, interactive stingray adventure. There are roughly seventy stingrays and they all have names and are identified by their distinctive personalities. The stingrays have had their barbs manicured and groomed back by Disney's "marine specialists" for the protection of the guests. A portion of the proceeds from each excursion is donated directly to the Disney Conservation Fund.

Where Are The Horses? Originally, the island was going to include horseback riding on prepared trails like the bike path but the plan was cancelled when the concern was raised of how to evacuate the animals from the island in the event of a disaster like a hurricane.

Snorkeling Treasures. In the twenty-two acre snorkeling lagoon, swimmers can find by the orange buoys treasures including a sunken fishing boat, an anchor, a dive bell, a cannon and more while by the white buoys are the statue of Minnie Mouse laying on an ornate pedestal, Mickey Mouse as the figurehead on the prow of a ship with one arm raised high in the air, and the exterior hull of Captain Nemo's Nautilus submarine from the extinct 20,000 Leagues attraction at Walt Disney World.

The Post Office. The post office on the island is an actual functioning Bahamian post office with special Bahamian postage sold there and a "Castaway Cay" postmark. Postcards can be purchased at the gift shops on the island or on the ship. The Post Office is located conveniently just a few feet down the path from the ship on the right hand side on the way to the Tram Stop.

According to the back story, the manager is May B. Tamara ("maybe tomorrow") that may help explain that it may take weeks for a postcard mailed from the site to arrive in the United States. In addition, the hours for the post office vary.

On August 1, 1998, the Bahamas issued two fifty-five cent postage stamps (daytime and nighttime) depicting Castaway Cay and a ship representing the Disney Cruise Line. Today, the cost of a stamp is sixty-five cents and can be purchased at Guest Services on the ship as well as at the post office. Bahamian postage must be used to mail a postcard from this location.

First Wedding. The first DCL hosted wedding on Castaway Cay took place on Valentine's Day, February 14, 1999.

Legend of Castaway Cay. The DCL produced a photo album in 2005 that was designed like a vintage Dell comic book with a cover of Donald hanging by ropes painting the outside of a cruise ship while Huey threatens to cut one of the ropes.

Inside besides sleeves for photos was a two page comic book story entitled *Legend of Castaway Cay*.

Donald and his three nephews arrive at Castaway Cay and discuss whether there is treasure on the island. As they disembark they meet Mickey Mouse and Minnie in their cruise ship outfits. Goofy dressed as a sailor welcomes them to Scuttle's Cove as Daisy Duck decides to go to Serenity Bay for a private beach massage.

Donald smells barbecue but his nephews convince him to go snorkeling where they encounter a "legendary Buenarian Bubble fish". Donald tries to intimidate the fish out of his way and it retaliates by blowing a huge bubble that engulfs Donald and send him to the surface. A passing seagull bursts the bubble and the explosion sends Donald smashing into Pete who is on the stern of the ship doing some painting.

The final panel has Pete saying, "Them's that messes up the job, does the job...or else!" Donald is hanging by the ropes with paint brushes and Huey threatening to cut one of the ropes. Donald grumbles, "Blasted bubble fish! Things like that never happen to The Little Mermaid!"

Hurricanes. Because Castaway Cay is located in a storm area it is not unexpected for hurricanes to hit it. At the end of 2004 Hurricanes Frances and Jeanne hit the island hard. About 90% of the facilities were destroyed. Due to the effects of Frances and Jeanne the entire bay had to be dredged and rebuilt. All of the underwater snorkel trail had to be remade due to the storm surge in the bay.

Hurricane Dorian. On August 28, 2019, the National Hurricane Center estimated that a major hurricane would impact an area including the private islands belonging to several cruise lines.

Royal Caribbean International evacuated 400 staff members from its island, CocoCay, MSC Cruises evacuated 600 construction workers from its soon-to-open Ocean Cay island and Carnival evacuated its staff from its Half Moon Cay island prior to the storm.

Disney Cruise Line decided to leave its staff on Castaway Cay, to ride out the storm in the company's hurricane shelter. One hundred and two staff members stayed in the concrete shelter, which the company said is 20 feet above sea level and designed to withstand a Category 5 hurricane.

All crew members remained safe during the storm and the company said no one was injured.

"Having operated Castaway Cay for more than 20 years, we have extensive experience managing situations like this, with the care and safety of our Crew driving every decision we make," wrote Kim Prunty, a spokesperson for Disney Cruise Line.

When Dorian struck, Castaway Cay was the cruise line island located closest to the center of the storm. The Category 5 hurricane hovered over nearby Grand Bahama and the Abaco islands for two days, pummeling them with 165 mph winds and creating storm surges as high as 23 feet. Dorian was the most powerful hurricane in recorded history to hit the Bahamas.

What's in a Name on Castaway Cay? On Castaway Cay there is some authentic signage like a vintage one on the side of a building of the Lone Ranger promoting Merita Bread.

However, there is also signage purposely made to look antique and authentic but are really tributes to Disney personnel just like the windows on Main Street in the Leaving the ship, on the left side there is a sign proclaiming: "Captain Bob Iger. Shrimp Distributors. Quality. Reliability. Key West. Willow Bay." Iger, of course, is the Chairman and Chief Executive Officer of the Walt Disney Company.

On the right hand side is the Pump House with lettering stating: "Bob Chapek. Master Ship Builder." Chapek is Chairman of Disney Parks, Experiences and Products and some people suspect he may become the next CEO after Iger.

Outside of Cookie's Too is a sign saying "T. Skees and Co. Purveyor of Finest Seafood". Imagineer Theron Skees has been with WDI for over twenty years which is pretty impressive these days and oversaw work on Pirates of the Caribbean at Disneyland Paris, helped oversee the opening of Hong Kong Disneyland and oversaw the transformation of Downtown Disney into Disney Springs. In 2016, he was appointed the new portfolio creative lead for the Disney Cruise Line.

Another sign had "Seaside Fresh. James Urry. The Webster Cannery Co. Family Owned and Operated for 40 Years". With more than 35 years of cruise entertainment experience, Urry joined Disney Cruise Line in September 1999 to launch the Disney Wonder as cruise director. He has been involved in the conception creating and implementation of all shipboard entertainment and programming components for the fleet.

In his current role as Vice President of entertainment and port adventures for Disney Cruise Line, Jim Urry is responsible for the total onboard entertainment and age-specific activities for adults, families and children, and also shore excursions.

Another sign says "Atlantic Trawling Co. Pat Gerrity. Shrimp Distributors Est. 1902". Patrick Gerrity is Director of Safety Environmental Division, Disney Cruise Vacations Inc.

The colorful crates by the side of the bathroom include some fun references as well including: Lost Boy Maps, Belle's Books and Peter's Pans.

At one time there was a "Capt. Tom Staggs & Sons. Towing and Salvage. Quality. Reliability. Key West. Canaveral." sign. Tom Staggs was the Chief Operating Officer for the Walt Disney Company but left in 2016.

Outside on the corner of the She Sells shop is still a sign for "Chandlery and General Store. Fisherman's Friend M. Ouimet Proprieter" that is a reference to Matt Ouimet who was DCL president in 1999 and served as President of Disneyland during its 50th anniversary celebration. He left the Walt Disney Company in 2006 to take the role of President, Hotel Group with Starwood Hotels and Resorts.

Monstro Point. Monstro Point is a reference to themenacing whale in the animated feature *Pinocchio* (1940) who was gigantic enough to swallow entire ships. The name Monstro means "monster" in Portuguese and archaic Italian. In the movie he was primarily animated by Wolfgang Reitherman and his growls provided by Thurl Ravenscroft. Monstro Point, located at Scuttle's Cove, is a sandy play area for children featuring a "whale dig" site complete with jumbo-sized whale bones.

Lighthouse Point

With the DCL fleet preparing to almost double its size, Disney decided to obtain another island besides Castaway Cay.

The southern point of the Bahamian island of Eleuthera has white-sand beaches, limestone bluffs, and clear blue water. Disney has announced it will develop 746 acres of this 110 mile long island to develop a port with a pier, shops, a marina, restaurants and walkways through a nearby forest and around salt ponds.

It is located fifty miles east of Nassau and is part of a collection known by Bahamians as the Family Islands. It is roughly sixty miles away from Castaway Cay.

Disney's plan was initially opposed by a local non-profit group of Bahamian environmentalists who proposed a different plan for the area, resulting in violent, divisive tensions among the local 11,000 residents.

An organization called One Eleuthera Foundation wanted the land designated a national park with tourism attractions (including canoe rentals, a dive center and horseback tours) and worried that the Disney project would block local access to the beaches and a historic lighthouse on the southern point.

In addition, the group argued that most of the revenue generated under Disney's plan would go to the cruise line, with only a small amount of jobs and tax revenues staying on the island.

Jeff Vahle, president of Disney Cruise Line, responded:

> We have approached this project with a focus on protecting and sustaining the natural beauty of this historic location, creating quality jobs and economic opportunities for Bahamians, and celebrating the unique culture of the Family Islands.

Vahle published an op-ed article that appeared in several Bahamian newspapers, promising that its project would preserve more of the land than some previous proposals by others that called for hundreds of homes, condominiums, hotels and a 140-slip marina.

Disney has already signed an agreement to purchase the land from a private international developer — estimated by locals to be priced at more than $25 million — but still needed approval from the commonwealth's government before the property changed hands and the port developed.

A fact sheet distributed by Disney Cruise Line stated that the Disney proposal would create up to 150 jobs, would give locals access to the property and turn over 170 acres of the land to the government for conservation. In addition, one hundred acres of salt ponds would be preserved. It was also proven that Disney's operation of Castaway Cay pumped money into the economy.

In August 2019 at the D23 Expo, Bob Chapek, Chairman Disney Parks, Experiences & Products announced that the conflicts had been resolved and Disney Imagineer Joe Rohde, Portfolio Creative Executive Walt Disney Imagineering, was leading the development of this port

At the event, Rohde said Disney will be relying on local artists, local culture, and local food to create an experience that honors and celebrates the local Bahamian culture. He emphasized that Disney's presence on the island would be done in the same vein as Disney's Aulani Resort in Hawaii that he also supervised with special consideration of the local environment, peoples, and cultures.

Rohde stated:

> Lighthouse Point is the very southern most tip of the island of Eleuthera. It has these strange eroded cliff forms along the edge of the ocean, these different beaches, scooping coves that face this turquoise blue Bahamian kind of water and it's really spectacular.
>
> So the project is based on two inspirations. One is the living nature of the Lighthouse Point itself. The second inspiration is cultural where we are going to take a local idea, local people, local feelings, local stories and bring them to life at the place.
>
> But to make them authentic, we have to do that together with Bahamian artists and Bahamian thinkers and people from the Bahamian community. There will be a storytelling experience, musical experiences that all come together to make this very unique, vibrant, colorful art. So that when you arrive you feel like

"Oh, I've arrived at this actual place." Of course with the volume turned up, you have this really intense kind of experience.

The Bahamas offers a fascinating multi-cultural tradition of food, music, dance and storytelling. Eleuthera in particular is home to many artists and we will be working with painters, sculptors, writers, storytellers, musicians, weavers and artists of every kind, much like we did with Aulani in Hawaii, to create a completely unique experience that is rooted in Bahamian culture and imbued with Disney magic.

The goal is not to create an artificial back story like a pirate hideout but to take advantage of the natural culture. The new destination will complement Castaway Cay but will veer from the former's WDI created back story and concentrate more on an actual experience representing "a seaside adventure camp".

Rohde said, "The Lighthouse Point site is so beautiful and so full of nature that we want to preserve this and use our designs to call attention to the extraordinary quality of the place itself — a place of natural beauty, with a rich and fascinating cultural tradition ... to create a unique destination that is rooted in Bahamian culture and imbued with Disney magic."

For the design to be influenced by both the natural environment of Lighthouse Point and the culture of Eleuthera and The Bahamas, DCL is working with the local creative community, including master artists Kevin Cooper and Antonius Roberts, to create an experience rooted in the history and nature of The Bahamas.

Rohde said that the contributions of many local Bahamian artists will allow art and nature to "combine with Disney magic" and create a destination "that can only exist in one place."

DCL created a dedicated website to keep the people of the Bahamas informed as to the progress of the project as well as Disney fans interested in the new location. According to the site Disney has, "completed its purchase of the Lighthouse Point property and signed a Heads of Agreement with the government of The Bahamas" but that commencement of construction is waiting on an environmental impact study.

Enco International (Bahamas) Ltd. (ENCO), was chosen through a competitive bid process to perform geotechnical investigations at Lighthouse Point—an important component of on-site environmental due diligence. The work will help determine the most appropriate building techniques to use pending the acceptance of the Environmental Impact Assessment and Environmental Management Plan that also align with Disney's commitment to the environment.

The geotechnical work was reviewed by The Bahamas Environment, Science & Technology (BEST) Commission, which offered no objections.

Jeff Vahle said:

> We are committed to maximizing Bahamian participation in this project, and our selection of ENCO for this significant work through a competitive bid process is the result of our ongoing efforts to build relationships with Bahamian companies. To date, we have met with more than 70 companies that have expressed interest in assisting with our construction needs and we will continue to build relationships with them. We look forward to working with ENCO to move this important work forward in a way that is consistent with our longstanding commitment to the environment.

In accordance with the plan, the geotechnical investigations will involve taking small core samples of sand and rock in places where structures will be built on land and over the water.

"Carlos Palacious, Managing Principal of ENCO said, "(Disney is) extremely focused on the details and, above all, dedicated to approaching the Lighthouse Point project with the best intentions and the utmost respect for preserving the environment and celebrating the natural beauty of the site."

ENCO hired approximately half of its work crew from Eleuthera. Economic activity also will be generated in Eleuthera in the form of accommodations and other needs for crew members coming from other Bahamian islands during the approximately four-month duration of the work.

Disney has committed to develop less than 20 percent of the property; employ sustainable building practices, including an open-trestle pier that eliminates the need to dredge a ship channel; establish environmental monitoring programs during construction and operation; donate more than 190 acres of privately owned land to the people of The Bahamas; and provide conservation education to employees, guests and vendors to ensure they know their role in protecting the site, among other commitments.

Through the Disney Conservation Fund, Disney has provided more than $13 million to marine conservation programs around the globe, including several in The Bahamas. Since 2007, Disney has been directly involved in leading a multiyear initiative to protect and rehabilitate coral reefs in The Bahamas and will continue to work with leading conservation organizations and communities to protect special places there.

Disney expects to invest $250-$400 million to create its island destination on Eleuthera. The site also talks about potential job creation for Bahamian residents both during construction and once the location is open.

Lighthouse Point is located on a peninsula known for its natural beauty and the plans on the website reveal large areas dedicated to conservation. Guests will be able to learn about the Bahamian culture and conservation effort at an art and culture center, walk through pedestrian nature trails, or view the island from above via the Adventure Camp trails and lookout towers.

From the look of the map, Lighthouse Point will feature access to four beach areas. Dining facilities and a Spa & Wellness Center are planned along with cabanas for those wishing a more private experience.

Another detail revealed is the location of the access pier to the island. As Disney pioneered with its first private island, Castaway Cay, the ships can dock and unload to a pier, rather than requiring tenders from the ship. Additionally, rather than dredging a ship channel, Lighthouse Point will feature a long pier out into deeper waters. Guests will be able to catch a tram to their destination at a depot just steps from the ship instead of having to walk the length of the pier.

About the Author

Jim Korkis is an internationally respected Disney historian who has written hundreds of articles and thirty books about all things Disney over the last forty years. Jim grew up in Glendale, California where starting at the young age of fifteen, he was able to meet and interview some of Walt's original team of animators and Imagineers.

While Jim does not suffer from thalassophobia (fear of large bodies of water that appear vast, dark, deep, dangerous and far from land), he is much more comfortable with his feet on dry land even though he grew up frequenting the beaches and piers of Southern California.

In 1995, Jim relocated to Orlando, Florida where he worked for Walt Disney World in a variety of capacities including Entertainment, Animation, Disney Institute, Disney University, College and International Programs, Disney Cruise Line, Disney Design Group, Disney Vacation Club, Disney Learning Center, Yellow Shoes Marketing and more.

His original research on Disney history has been used often by the Disney Company as well as other organizations including the Disney Family Museum.

Several websites currently feature Jim's articles about Disney history:
- MousePlanet.com
- AllEars.net
- Yesterland.com
- CartoonResearch.com
- YourFirstVisit.net

In addition, Jim is a frequent guest on multiple podcasts as well as a consultant and keynote speaker to various businesses, schools and groups.

Jim is not currently an employee of the Disney Company.

To read more stories by Jim Korkis about Disney history, check out his other books, all available from ThemeParkPress.com.

- *The Vault of Walt, Volume 8, Christmas Edition (2019)*
- *Disney Never Lands (2019)*
- *Secret Stories of Extinct Disneyland (2019)*
- *The Unofficial Walt Disney World 1971 Companion (2019)*
- *The Vault of Walt: Volume 7, Christmas Edition (2018)*
- *Secret Stories of Mickey Mouse (2018)*
- *More Secret Stories of Disneyland (2018)*
- *Extra Secret Stories of Walt Disney World (2018)*
- *Call Me Walt (2017)*
- *Walt's Words (2017)*
- *Other Secret Stories of Walt Disney World (2017)*
- *Secret Stories of Disneyland (2017)*
- *The Vault of Walt: Volume 6 (2017)*
- *Gremlin Trouble (2017)*
- *Donald Duck's Daddy (2017)*
- *More Secret Stories of Walt Disney World (2016)*
- *The Vault of Walt: Volume 5 (2016)*
- *The Unofficial Disneyland 1955 Companion (2016)*
- *How to Be a Disney Historian (2016)*
- *Secret Stories of Walt Disney World (2015)*
- *The Vault of Walt: Volume 4 (2015)*
- *Everything I Know I Learned from Disney Animated Features (2015)*
- *The Vault of Walt: Volume 3 (2014)*
- *Animation Anecdotes (2014)*
- *Who's the Leader of the Club? Walt Disney's Leadership Lessons (2014)*
- *The Book of Mouse (2013)*
- *The Vault of Walt: Volume 2 (2013)*
- *Who's Afraid of the Song of the South? (2012)*
- *The Revised Vault of Walt (2012)*

About Theme Park Press

Theme Park Press publishes books primarily about the Disney company, its history, culture, films, animation, and theme parks, as well as theme parks in general.

Our authors include noted historians, animators, Imagineers, and experts in the theme park industry.

We also publish many books by first-time authors, with topics ranging from fiction to theme park guides.

And we're always looking for new talent. If you'd like to write for us, or if you're interested in the many other titles in our catalog, please visit:

www.ThemeParkPress.com

Theme Park Press Newsletter

Subscribe to our free email newsletter and enjoy:

- Free book downloads and giveaways
- Access to excerpts from our many books
- Announcements of forthcoming releases
- Exclusive additional content and chapters
- And more good stuff available nowhere else

To subscribe, visit www.ThemeParkPress.com, or send email to newsletter@themeparkpress.com.

Read more about these books
and our many other titles at:

www.ThemeParkPress.com

Printed in Great Britain
by Amazon